ONE SIGNAL
PUBLISHERS
————
ATRIA

MERKEL'S LAW

WISDOM FROM THE WOMAN WHO LED THE FREE WORLD

MELISSA EDDY

ONE SIGNAL
PUBLISHERS

——

ATRIA

New York   London   Toronto   Sydney   New Delhi

ATRIA

An Imprint of Simon & Schuster, LLC
1230 Avenue of the Americas
New York, NY 10020

First One Signal Publishers/Atria Books hardcover edition August 2024

ONE SIGNAL PUBLISHERS / ATRIA BOOKS and colophon are trademarks of Simon & Schuster, LLC

Simon & Schuster: Celebrating 100 Years of Publishing in 2024

For information about special discounts for bulk purchases, please contact Simon & Schuster Special Sales at 1-866-506-1949 or business@simonandschuster.com.

The Simon & Schuster Speakers Bureau can bring authors to your live event. For more information or to book an event, contact the Simon & Schuster Speakers Bureau at 1-866-248-3049 or visit our website at www.simonspeakers.com.

Interior design by Jill Putorti

Manufactured in the United States of America

1 3 5 7 9 10 8 6 4 2

Library of Congress Cataloging-in-Publication Data has been applied for.

ISBN 978-1-9821-9103-0
ISBN 978-1-9821-9105-4 (ebook)

CONTENTS

MERKEL'S LAW

INTRODUCTION

Applause, peppered with cheers, rolled through the crowd gathered beneath the crimson banners and newly green leaves of the trees on Harvard Yard. From a podium on a stage before the wall of sound, the woman dressed in a bright, turquoise-blue blazer looked up from her speech at the crowd before her. One by one, they were jumping to their feet. She pursed her lips, allowing a brief look of annoyance to cross her face. Then she raised her right hand, as if she could physically stop the cheering. Instead, row after row of parents, professors, and students stood up, the steady rhythm of their clashing palms reverberating off the brick walls that frame Harvard Yard. No one on that afternoon in 2019 appeared interested in keeping protocol by allowing the speaker to finish her speech within the time allotted.

What the audience wanted was to celebrate the woman that many saw as a lone defender of the brand of liberal democracy they had long considered their American birthright. In the past months they had seen the Mueller report on Russian interference in the 2016 election, a fierce debate over whether to impeach the president, and a series of squabbles with some of America's oldest allies—including Germany, a democracy shaped by the influence of the United States after Hitler's defeat in World War II. The collective relief of hearing a leader praise the principles of democracy, multilateralism, and respect for others' history, identity, and religion buzzed through the crowd. Angela Merkel looked up and beamed.

She may have given little thought to being crowned "The World's Most Powerful Woman" by *Forbes* magazine ten times between 2006 and 2018—First Lady Michelle Obama interrupted her streak in 2010—and personally rejected the moniker Chancellor of the Free World, but the audience was not having it. In the woman who stood before them listing the values around which she had oriented her life and led her country for nearly four full terms, they recognized an individual who remained impervious to the petty fights on social media, respected facts, and refused to give in to bullies, and whose faith in democracy traced its roots to an understanding of life in its absence. They kept on clapping.

Merkel had long been uncomfortable with adoration or attempts to celebrate her person or achievements. She routinely met cheering from members of her own political party, whether celebrating her as their leader with more than 90 percent support or rejoicing at another four years in the chancellery, with the same response: a smile and a speech, followed by a wave and a quick exit from the stage. When she was a teenager, mopping up her much-older rivals in the Russian-language competition—an important event at her high school in the former East Germany, which answered to Moscow—her teacher had to remind the young Angela to smile and look pleased when she won. Decades later, the political system around her had changed, but even during her earliest years in politics, aides would remind her to smile, to give a bit back to the crowd.

Connecting with the public was never Merkel's strength. An aide told me Merkel was jealous when Barack Obama, then a junior senator, drew a crowd of two hundred thousand for a speech in central Berlin, fully aware that not half as many would turn out to hear her speak. Yet Merkel brought her own magnetism first to the German and then the world political stage.

"Unique, incomparable, inimitable" is how Christine Lagarde, her friend and peer, described Merkel.[1]

Her approach to power was shaped by her analytical mind, sharpened by more than a decade spent as a research scientist, combined with a willingness to listen to others. She stubbornly insisted on seeking compromise; regardless of how intractable a problem appeared, she refused to quit until a compromise had been hammered out. Raised within the confines of a political system that sought to impose its will on people, she was driven by her belief that individuals thrived in an environment that allowed them to push themselves. She set out to test the limits of her own abilities and in doing so wound up defining a generation.

———

From the former East German leader who named her his spokeswoman only months after she had abandoned her microscope for politics in 1990, to the members of Germany's tradition-bound Christian Democratic Union, to the tens of thousands of voters who overcame their aversion to her political party's conservative roots to return her to a final four-year term in office in 2017, given her humanistic stance on migration from the Middle East, people trusted Angela Merkel.

It wasn't only the Germans. Merkel received a standing ovation after addressing the joint U.S. houses of Congress. President George W. Bush invited her for a personal visit to his family's ranch in Texas. President Obama awarded her the Presidential Medal of Freedom, the highest civilian recognition in the United States. India recognized her with the Jawaharlal Nehru Prize for International Understanding—she used the proceeds to set up a scholarship for Indian law students studying in Germany. Europe honored her with its Charlemagne Prize. Merkel stole French hearts by breaking out her best French to set a hundred-year-old woman straight that *"je suis la chancelière allemande,"* the German chancellor, not President Emmanuel Macron's wife, as the French president awarded her his country's highest recognition, the Grand Cross of the Legion of Honor.

Academics, scholars, and scientists also looked up to Merkel. A physicist by training, she earned her doctorate in the field and spent more than a decade in research, before switching to politics. But the years spent testing theories and analyzing the results stayed with her long after she left the laboratory. They informed her approach to decision-making and cemented her faith in the belief that while politicians and business leaders could and would bend truths to fit their narratives, the laws of physics and science endured. More than a dozen of the world's leading institutes of higher education (Johns Hopkins, Stanford, Hebrew University in Jerusalem, and Peking University in Beijing) showered her with honorary degrees. Harvard Law School had topped its award by inviting her to join the ranks of Benazir Bhutto, Ellen Johnson Sirleaf, Oprah Winfrey, and several former U.S. presidents in giving the commencement address to its graduating class.

The university had wanted the fiercely private chancellor to invoke some lessons drawn from her own life. Merkel, ever the diligent student, delivered. Among her call to support multilateralism and free trade among nations, she wove in references to Germany's responsibility for sparking World War II. As she warned of the challenges posed by a rapidly warming climate and cautioned that unchecked advances in technology could pose a threat, she joked that the cell phones most students held in their pockets ran faster than the computers built by engineers in the Soviet Union that were considered cutting-edge when she was carrying out research for her PhD.

Not once in her thirty-five-minute address did Merkel mention President Donald Trump by name. Rarely had Merkel ever responded to the barbs fired off by the man who became the forty-fifth U.S. president, reaching back to 2015, when he posted to Twitter that instead of choosing him, *Time* magazine had named the "person who is ruining

Germany" as its Person of the Year. She knew that she didn't have to mention Trump. When she urged students not to "always act on our first impulses," but instead to "take a moment to stop, be still, think, pause," laughter rippled through the rows of people seated in the wooden folding chairs before her. As at that time the U.S. president often seemed to be governing through unfiltered, brief messages fired off over social media at all hours of the night and day, the intended target of chancellor's advice could not have been clearer.

But Merkel had not come up with that idea only for the speech; she lived it. At key moments in her steady climb to the chancellery through the ranks of Germany's male-dominated political system, she had always maintained that ability to retreat into herself, whether physically withdrawing to her modest country home in the region where she grew up, or just conferring with aides in her office, reading over the folders of notes and polling results to figure out where the public stood. Only then, armed with the facts and the options that she had weighed against one another, would she make a decision. To some of her peers and the public, including journalists eager for details and descriptions that inform governing, Merkel's tightly guarded interior processes could be frustrating. But in an age of oversharing, when the scramble for scoops and the tsunami of friends' and acquaintances' personal details spilled onto social media sites became too much to absorb, her refusal to be rushed or give up more information than she deemed necessary also came across as inspirational. Silence in the face of noise and willingness not just to talk, but first to listen and think, served as the trademarks of her power.

Merkel's mother had instilled the power of silence into her children from the day they started school. Merkel grew up when Germany was split into two countries, a division of powers that followed the defeat of Adolf Hitler and the end of World War II. Merkel was born in West Germany, which was allied with the United States, and her father was a pastor in the Lutheran Church who felt called to bring the word of God to the people on the other side of the Iron Curtain, to East Germany, an authoritarian state under the influence of the Soviet Union. For the first thirty-five years of her life, the power of the state and the limitations it imposed on her public life taught her lessons that influenced her personal journey, from her decision to study science, a realm she considered impervious to the government's propaganda, to her decision to seize on the upheaval ushered in by the fall of the Berlin Wall to move into politics—a profession that she approached as an act of service, first to her political party, later to her country. In her message to the Harvard graduates in 2019, she stressed another of the philosophies on which she had built her career, an idea rooted in her life experience of embracing the unexpected change unleashed upon her world when the Berlin Wall fell in 1989, presenting her with previously unimaginable opportunities. "Let's surprise ourselves by showing what is possible. Let us surprise ourselves with what we can do!"[2]

Merkel had used the same phrase in her first address to the German parliament in 2005, speaking to her country as the first-ever woman chancellor—and the first to hail from the formerly Communist-run part of the country. That she found herself standing at the head of the German government had surprised many people in Germany, the United States, and its allies. Merkel had bested her cigar-chomping predecessor, Gerhard Schröder, by only the narrowest margin, and he had initially refused to accept defeat. Many people, including some within Merkel's own party, did not think she was up to the job of steering the world's third-largest economy—Germany had a GDP of $2.9 trillion at the time—out of the doldrums that had led it to be dubbed the Sick Man of Europe. Never before had a woman held so much power in Europe's largest country, a founding member of the European Union. The closest comparison was Margaret Thatcher, a fellow leader of her country's conservative party with a weakness for fashionable handbags. Attempts to draw parallels between the two leaders quickly evaporated as it became apparent that Merkel's analytical, consensus-driven approach to leadership differed greatly from

Thatcher's hardfisted adherence to free-market principles. But when Merkel demanded that Greece undergo painful economic cuts to pull Europe out of a debilitating debt crisis in 2009, many likened her hard stance to Thatcher's busting of Britain's unions. Like Thatcher before her, Merkel became known as the new Iron Lady.

The seeming need to borrow monikers bestowed on previous female leaders reflected how exceptional it was, and still is today, for a woman to be the head of government in the world's leading industrialized nations. It is an achievement that no American woman has yet reached. Hillary Clinton came the closest when she ran against Trump in 2016. When Merkel came to power, she was only the second woman to lead a country considered one of the world's top ten industrialized nations, after Thatcher. Halfway into her first term in office, Merkel traveled to Liberia to meet with President Ellen Johnson Sirleaf, the first woman elected as leader of an African nation. Their unique situations cemented what Merkel called a "political friendship" and sparked a fascination with Africa that would follow her throughout her chancellorship. Overall, Europeans have been more willing to elect women as their leaders, as have Latin Americans and Southeast Asians. But when Merkel stepped down, she left the world's most powerful countries all in the hands of men.

Before her election, Merkel's looks were fair game. German reporters routinely commented on the dullness of her page-boy hairstyle, the length of her skirts, and her choice of shoes. In the United States we were more restrained, if not much better. As a journalist covering the conflict in Kosovo for the Associated Press in 1999, I had a memorable phone call with an editor in New York when First Lady Hillary Clinton visited a refugee camp in Macedonia. My editor's first question to me was "What is she wearing?" In the run-up to the 2005 German election, having seen groups of woman organize around Merkel with the idea of backing one of their own for the country's highest political position, I suggested writing a story looking at how German women felt about the prospect of a female chancellor and what influence gender could have on the vote. My male editors shot it down as sexist. Over time, that changed, as did my employer.

By the time I moved to the *New York Times* in 2012, the world had not only become increasingly fascinated with Merkel's political achievements, but also with her personal background, motivation, and style of leadership. Gender was a rising topic of interest, covered not only in the *Times*, but in countless blogs and podcasts dedicated to exploring how the issue played out in the world. Discussions about a female politician's choice of clothing or hairstyle were becoming increasingly rare in the media, unless as a point of how clothing could be used to convey power. Women themselves were also understanding the messages that could be transmitted through style. Merkel was no exception. As she grew more comfortable in her power, Merkel had taken command of her look by inventing her own uniform of sorts—a combination of brightly colored blazers paired with black pants. It was a style so simple that it rendered questions of her choice of dress unremarkable, save for those of us Merkel watchers who tried to decipher the color-coded signals that she sent through which shade of blazer she was wearing on any given day. Black was for somber, serious events; blue, her favorite color, for celebrations; and red when she wanted to flex her power. But to most, Merkel's blazer choice became as uninteresting as the shade of her male counterparts' ties. The only time this changed was for formal events, where she had no qualms about turning up year in, year out, in previously worn designs. Years before recycling became a fashion, Merkel was brazenly re-wearing her favorite pieces without a second thought. (Her trademark suits landed in the local bin for recycled clothes.)

By 2016, Merkel may have succeeded in changing how people in her own country viewed her—no longer as a unique exception, but as a politician subject to the same cycle of criticism and praise as any previous chancellor. But the outside world saw her differently. Especially in the United States, where the combination of polarization amplified through social media led to a breakdown in public discourse. Merkel's refusal to stoop to a level of incivility she considered unacceptable caught the attention of countless Americans. When Donald Trump called her "insane" and the "woman who is ruining Germany" during his 2016 campaign, she refused to engage. Privately, Merkel was shocked that the leader of a country she had long admired for its staunch opposition to the authoritarian, centralized state where she grew up could be heading in such a direction. But if her life as the daughter of a pastor in a country that deeply distrusted the church or her experience as the only woman in a physics department dominated by male professors and students had taught her anything, it was to keep focused on her work and her thoughts to herself. Those skills had steeled her against the male politicians who had dismissed her as little more than the protégé of her mentor, German chancellor Helmut Kohl, dubbing her "Kohl's girl."

She had already coped with trying to find a women's bathroom on her first visit to the Middle East—she had to use a men's room while her staff stood guard—and holding in her unease around dogs as Russian president Vladimir Putin's black Lab sniffed at her legs during a press conference while he looked on, feigning innocence. Even many Germans had forgotten that before she could take her first oath of office, Merkel had had to repeatedly remind her predecessor—and members of her own party—that the rules of play in German politics dictate that the candidate for the party with the most votes becomes chancellor, a point that her predecessor seemed to have forgotten when faced with having to concede defeat by a woman.

As I watched this woman bat away insults and grow in confidence so strong that by 2013 she campaigned for her third term in office on the simple, confident slogan "You know me," I found myself contemplating whether it was time for me to return to the United States. More than a decade had passed since I arrived in Berlin as a Fulbright scholar. My marriage had collapsed and I faced the prospect of raising two children on my own in a foreign country. The idea of returning home to be near family looked increasingly attractive. But to maintain my career would have meant working in a big city, such as New York. I knew friends there who were paying the same amount in childcare for one child, for one week, that I was paying for two children in a month.

The woman I had to thank for this kind of affordable childcare was Angela Merkel. She had laid the groundwork for the law in the 1990s, when she served as minister for families and youth in the first government of reunified Berlin. Although childless, she had grown up in a system where women were expected to work, and the state helped to make that possible. Merkel's guarantees of access to affordable childcare reflected her ability to lead by example. It would take years before she could concede to the demands of feminists to acknowledge that she belonged in their camp, but throughout her career, she quietly sought ways to promote women and girls, without ever outwardly making it a talking point. This angered many women, especially Germans, who pointed to the persistent lack of representation of women in business and the shrinking number of female lawmakers in the German parliament during Merkel's sixteen years in power. Some women praised Merkel for leading by example, but to others she had failed to use her position to tackle persistent issues of inequality, from the gender pay gap, with German women earning 20 percent less than men in equivalent positions in 2019, to not setting laws requiring gender parity in positions of power. Debates over whether Merkel should have supported Ukraine joining NATO back in 2008 or had demanded too much austerity from Greece during the European financial crisis could have occurred with any German chancellor, but the criticism over her reluctance to embrace feminism reflected the seemingly impossible demands imposed on women leaders. Once a woman is in office, representation is not enough. It is a challenge that none of her male counterparts have ever had to face.

Angela Merkel was not only Germany's first woman chancellor, or *Kanzlerin*, she was also its first to be born after World War II and the first to hail from the former Communist-run country of East Germany. Under her leadership, the country that she helped reunite emerged from the shadow of its post–World War II division and learned to balance acknowledgement of past wrongs with pride in present achievements. Merkel oversaw the passing of a minimum wage and opened the doors for same-sex marriage. She put climate change, world hunger, and women's rights on the agenda of the world's leading industrial countries. She forged a consensus that held the European Union together through a financial crisis.

When it came to Germany's soft power, Merkel engendered a new reputation for her country on the world stage. She was helped by her unbridled enthusiasm for soccer. Images of her in the stadium, arms raised in excitement while cheering the national soccer team when her country hosted the 2006 World Cup, helped inspire a newfound pride in being German. A new generation unencumbered by the Cold War divisions that had darkened Merkel's opportunities as a young person felt no shame in painting their faces in the black-red-gold of the country's flag and rooting for their national team with an energy to match that of their chancellor. Over four weeks, positively giddy Germans welcomed fans from across the globe to their beer gardens and outdoor broadcasts of the games in parks and blocked off roads that reverberated with a street-fair atmosphere that became known as "public viewings." The Germans even seemed to surprise themselves with their ability to celebrate their team's third-place finish with almost as much enthusiasm as if they had won the championship. That summer of soccer was Merkel's first in office and set the tone for how much of the world viewed her chancellorship. In Germany it's known as the *"Summer Fairy Tale."*

Nearly a decade later, Germans drew on that same spirit of open-hearted generosity when people fleeing the conflicts in Syria and Afghanistan began making their way to Germany on foot, carrying little more than their cell phones and the clothes on their backs. When Merkel decided to allow thousands of people who had been trapped in the main train station in Budapest, Hungary, to make their way to Munich, crowds turned out to welcome them with food, toys, and banners. After decades of being haunted by the memories of the people they had chased from their country or murdered in gas chambers, Germans embraced the chance to do the right thing. Although sentiment among part of the population soon tipped against the new arrivals, Merkel never wavered in her resolution that she had made the right decision, the humanitarian one. "I have to say quite honestly, if we now start having to apologize for showing a friendly face in emergency situations, then this is not my country."

Under Merkel, Germany emerged from the shadow of its World War II caricature as the world's bad guy, driven by evil and nationalism. Throughout her sixteen years in power Germany came to be seen as a modern, open nation, unafraid to take risks. A country respected for and respectful of individuality, but not at the price of the overall welfare of society. Above all, the world saw Germany as a leading democracy, a country that embraced freedom and challenged everyone who lived there to become who they imagined they could be. This rebranding of her country is one of Merkel's greatest, yet most overlooked achievements, one that resonates in her absence as Germany's partners look to Berlin for leadership in the crises from the Middle East to Ukraine. Pope Francis summed up the shift her country had undergone by praising Merkel as a humane leader capable of commanding attention at home and abroad. "Her word carries international weight," he said. "Her policies are good for Germany and for the global world."[3]

When they jumped to their feet that May afternoon after Merkel had called on the graduates to "tear down walls of ignorance and narrow-mindedness, for nothing has to stay as it is," the audience in Harvard Yard were thinking of the fractured political moment that was the United States of America in spring 2019. Not Merkel. She remembered watching her mother cry the morning the Berlin Wall went up and the euphoria she experienced slipping unhindered through a checkpoint to the other side the night that it came down. Her life had taught her to embrace moments when the ground seemed to be shifting beneath her feet, having understood they presented an opportunity for personal growth and improvement. This is one of the underlying lessons that helped to drive Merkel as a leader and a woman throughout her unique and remarkable career. I have selected this and several other principles that drove her, which can be viewed as lessons and applied by others seeking to lead on any level, or simply to live with integrity.

This work is informed by my having spent my own professional life following the chancellor, parsing her speeches and posing her questions throughout her sixteen years in office. It is also influenced by my experience of having lived in the country that she led, watching it change, and watching Germans change in their assessment of her. Although my job revolves around politics and the economy, this work is an attempt to look at Merkel as an individual and reflect on the influence that she had on my own life and the world that she helped to shape.

I've selected ten lessons, or what might be thought of as principles, that Merkel, a leader with remarkable consistency, has displayed time and again as tenets she returns to in times of crisis and of peace, and what have made her one of the most effective leaders of the twenty-first century.

Chapter 1

EVERYTHING I DO,
I DO AS A WOMAN

Then I am one, too.

—ANGELA MERKEL, RESPONDING TO
QUEEN MÁXIMA'S DEFINITION OF A FEMINIST, 2017

"Do you consider yourself a feminist?" It was the question that everyone in the room at the Women20 conference in 2017 had been burning to ask the woman recognized at that time as the leader of the liberal, Western world. She was sitting onstage flanked by powerful women, from Christine Lagarde, at the time head of the International Monetary Fund, Her Majesty Queen Máxima of the Netherlands, and Ivanka Trump, who was representing the United States.

Merkel, dressed in a bright red blazer over her standard uniform of black pants and chunky necklace of thick amber beads, squirmed as she contemplated her answer. Lagarde and Chrystia Freeland, the foreign minister of Canada, gleefully pumped their fists in the air and clapped as if cheering on their favorite sports team. A wave of expectation rippled through the largely female audience. All the woman present, who had looked up to Merkel as a trailblazer and an example of a woman who led with authority, waited with anticipation. The normally notoriously well-prepared chancellor struggled to find a response to a question that everyone else in the auditorium seemed more than ready to answer for her with a resounding "Yes!"

Then she began, as if arguing in a debate. "Okay. To be honest," Merkel said, before breaking into a smile as a swell of cheers rose from the crowd and her fellow panelists, believing the moment they had all been waiting for had finally arrived. We should have known better. After all, Merkel had risen to power by often resisting expectations that she fit a mold of any shape or form. She had stoically withstood months of withering criticism for her unbending attitude that Greece must not default and for her decision to keep Germany's borders open as hundreds of thousands of migrants arrived. Just because a roomful of women, many of them powerful and several of whom she counted as friends, wanted to hear her pronounce herself part of a movement they believed in and associated her with did not mean that she would just give in.

Instead, Merkel launched into a brief explanation of her understanding of the history of feminism. She pointed out the similarities and the differences she saw between herself and the movement for the emancipation and equality of women in Germany. Credit, she insisted, had to be given to those women who fought hard for representation, who took risks and openly battled against a society that preferred to keep them at home or in subordinate roles. In Merkel's eyes, they, and they alone, had earned the right to call themselves feminists.

"I do not want to decorate myself with a title that I do not have," Merkel said. She cited Alice Schwarzer, one of Germany's most important crusaders for women's rights, as an example of someone who could call herself a feminist because she took on the difficult battles to advance women's position in society. "I don't want to come along and rest on their success and say, 'Now I'm a feminist, that is great,'" Merkel said. Then sensing the mood, she added, "I am not afraid—if you find that I'm a feminist, take a vote." Hands shot up in the audience. "Okay. But I don't want to decorate myself with false feathers."[1]

The moderator then asked the seven other women on the panel if they considered themselves to be feminists, and five of them raised their hands. Merkel looked around, then almost seemed to pout, rejected and resigned to her fate. It was at that moment that Máxima, who was born in Argentina and worked in international finance in New York City before meeting the heir to the Dutch throne and becoming queen of one of Europe's wealthiest countries, spoke up. Until then, she had observed the debate, not raising her hand to the moderator's question. Instead she lifted her microphone. "What's in a name?" she asked, turning first to the moderator and then to the audience. Merkel turned toward the queen. Leaning over, she looked at Queen Máxima, who sat two chairs to Merkel's left, wearing a dress printed with poppies, which were the same bright color of Merkel's blazer.

"I just want that all women have freedom of choice, that they have opportunities that they can grab, and really be happy and proud of themselves and equal on every floor," Queen Máxima declared. "If that is a feminist, then I am a feminist."

Relieved that she had been offered an out to the situation and a definition broad enough that it could be embraced by men and women, or by anyone seeking equality and justice, Merkel smiled and resolutely declared, "Then I am one, too."

Four years later, sitting beside author and activist Chimamanda Ngozi Adichie, Merkel credited the Dutch queen, with her wide, inclusive definition of the term, for opening the door to feminism for her. "She pointed out to me that, at the core, isn't it about men and women being equal in participation in society and in all of life?" Merkel said. "And in that sense, I can affirm today that I am a feminist—we should all be feminists."[2] Again, the room erupted in cheers.

Angela Merkel tried hard throughout her term in office to downplay her gender, professing to be the chancellor for all Germans. That did little to change the reality that women and girls from across the globe looked up to and admired her for the very fact that for the better part of two decades she shaped the direction of one of the world's most powerful countries. No matter how the chancellor chose to define herself, everything she did, she did as a woman.

CAN A MAN BE CHANCELLOR?
THE IMPORTANCE OF ROLE MODELS

Early on in her chancellorship, the mere discussion of gender issues and whether Merkel intended to use her newly won position of power to help promote the status of women in Germany were delicate subjects. When confronted with such questions, Merkel would stress that she had been elected to represent "all people in Germany," not just those from the former East Germany, and not just women. That did not stop many German women, even those who did not like or traditionally support the conservative party, from supporting Merkel in order to break the glass ceiling with the expectation that she would further equality for women.

The Nazis' cult of motherhood had cast its long shadow over German society. Starting in the 1930s, women were encouraged to bear many children, even out of wedlock. Those who had more than four children were recognized with a special award, the Cross of Honor of the German Mother. After the war, it was the women who rolled up their sleeves to clear the rubble, paving the way for a new nation. But conservative traditions, such as schools letting out in time for children to go home for a hot lunch, and tax laws that rewarded single-earning households, soon crept back in, sending women back into their homes. After reunification, to the frustration of many East Germans, the more conservative, patriarchic societal norms from the wealthier West Germany became the default in the newly reunited nation. Tens of thousands of women from the East found themselves out of work, with no help or incentives to find a job. (Yet again, Merkel proved herself to be an exception, by moving into politics and rapidly rising through the ranks.)

As a result, Germany has remained further behind its European Union neighbors France and Denmark, along with the rest of Scandinavia, in representation of women in the workplace or positions of power. During Merkel's first campaign for the chancellery, a countess in

Germany's banking capital, Frankfurt, founded a group called Women
for Merkel. While most of those in the group belonged to Merkel's conservative party, the idea was to attract a more diverse group of women,
bound by a singular aim: to see one of their own in their country's
highest political office. Nearly two hundred women joined in the effort.
They made phone calls, canvassed, and organized rallies. Despite their
intention, they knew their country well enough to steer clear of flat-out
promoting Merkel simply because she was a woman. Instead of arguing
that Merkel as a woman could usher Germany into a new era, Women
for Merkel focused on her "credibility, reliability and a willingness to in-
novate" as the reason they would give her their vote, praising her "clear
mind" and ability to "dedicate herself fully to her tasks, whether as a
physicist, a minister."[3]

That was in 2005, when I was living in Frankfurt, working full-time
and realizing the challenge of finding adequate day care for my two children, then aged four and one. The preschool in our neighborhood was
able to take my older child from 9:00 a.m. to 11:00 a.m., but there was
no chance to get him into the afternoon care. The only option for my
infant daughter was to find a babysitter who could come and stay with
her every day.

Worse, most of my German friends didn't understand what the
problem was. At the time, German mothers commonly paused their
jobs and stayed home from work for three years, until their children
were old enough to be eligible for day care. But even then, most women
only returned to part-time work, to maintain flexibility for afternoon
childcare, which was not covered by day care or schools. What on the
surface looked like a generous offer, to my American eyes at least, was
in reality holding German women back from fully participating in the
workforce or building successful careers, since having two children or
more meant sitting out at least six years when they could have been
expanding their skill sets and growing their networks. Fathers were not
eligible for parental leave subsidies when Merkel became chancellor.

Even those who wanted to stay home with their children—and there weren't many—received no support from the government and risked losing their jobs.

Fortunately, my job moved me to Berlin, where I settled in a neighborhood in what was former East Berlin, just a couple of blocks from where Merkel had squatted in her first apartment after leaving her husband. Berlin had a remnant of the socialist system that had ruled the former East and an abundance of preschool and childcare centers, where I found spots for both of my children. Within her first three years as chancellor, Merkel's government passed a law guaranteeing a place in public day care for all children under three—she had proposed a law with a similar guarantee for preschoolers already in 1994 while serving as minister for family and youth. That law made it possible for me, as a single parent, to keep both my children in full-time day care for a monthly price roughly equivalent to what my friends back home in the United States were paying for one child per week. Knowing that my children were cared for gave me the flexibility to pursue my career as a foreign correspondent, covering Germany for some of the leading American news outlets.

It wasn't only in Germany that gender politics were sidelined. When I suggested to my editor at the Associated Press that I report and write a story about the women organizing on Merkel's behalf and explore whether women were planning on voting for her because she was a woman, the idea was shot down as "sexist" and "not relevant." By the time Merkel left office, we reporters were all writing stories about her impact on women in Germany. Society's view of what a woman could achieve and where she belonged had also changed. Annalena Baerbock, a member of the Greens who ran for chancellor in 2021, garnered almost no negative attention for her openly feminist position on several topics.

Still, many German women felt then and still feel that Merkel had not used her position to do enough to help them get ahead in politics and the workforce. While the number of women lawmakers in Germany's federal legislature, the Bundestag, rose steadily after reunification of the former East and West German states to nearly 36.5 percent in 2016, it fell back to less than 31 percent after the 2017 election, her final term in office.[4] During the sixteen years that Merkel held power, Germany plunged in international rankings for the number of women in national legislatures from sixteenth place to fifty-third, as other countries around the globe caught up.[5]

But representation in politics is only one aspect of empowerment. Across the board, the overall position of women in German society progressed under Merkel's tenure, according to statistics measured by the European Union's Institute for Gender Equality. Especially in terms of equal access to power for women, the country climbed steadily in its overall performance in education, economic and political influence, health care, and free time.[6]

What changed was in many ways more subtle, harder to define, but equally powerful. When Merkel's conservative party went looking for a candidate for the 2021 election campaign and only three men entered the running, the lack of a woman in the party she had led for eighteen years became national news. Leaving aside what this said about Merkel's ability to attract more women to her own party—the conservatives had traditionally been home to alpha males—that this gender imbalance was considered worthy of discussion in the nation's media reflected a profound shift from sixteen years earlier. Such a debate simply would not have happened before Merkel took power. Through her presence in the highest halls of power, Merkel, as a woman, fundamentally changed the way her own party, the media, and society thought about a woman's place in the world.

It wasn't always that easy. By the time Merkel left office, many Germans seemed to have forgotten the discussion that followed her narrow victory in 2005. Because she led by just four seats, the country's top newspapers floated suggestions that she should step aside to let a man from her party serve as chancellor. Even more extraordinary, they suggested that she should allow her challenger to remain in office for the first two of the four-year term, in what would amount to an unprecedented splitting of the chancellor's term. On the day that she raised her right hand to take the oath of office, Norbert Lammert, president of the German parliament, who administered the oath, dryly remarked, "Dear Dr. Merkel, this makes you the first democratically elected female head of government in Germany. This is a strong signal for many women and certainly for some men as well."[7]

But many of those men—the majority of Germany's political class—saw Merkel as little more than a seat warmer. Even within her own party, several of her male rivals viewed themselves as the rightful heirs to the chancellery. They figured it would just be a matter of time until Merkel faltered, paving the way for them to swoop in and take over, saving the day. Instead, she remained long enough for people to wonder, by the time she stepped down, whether a man could also do the job, a joke that Merkel enjoyed recounting: "No one laughs at a young girl today when she says she wants to be a minister or even chancellor when she grows up. There are even supposed to be questions about whether a man can also be chancellor, I am sometimes told."[8]

In her earliest years as a politician, Merkel often found herself the butt of jokes. Some made fun of her hairstyle or her clothes. Others took the form of disparaging monikers such as Kohl's girl and the German for mommy, *Mutti*. But all of them were based on demeaning her because of her gender. By the time she left office, Merkel had subtly flipped the jokes. The men jockeying to replace her found themselves trying to imitate the aura of calm competency that she exuded, insisting that their gender did not prevent them from being up to the job. It was not only the joke that had flipped. By refusing to even indulge the discussion surrounding her clothes, hair, or gender, Merkel had irrevocably altered how society viewed women and their role in the world. She had refused to change how she looked and who she was. Instead, using her infamous staying power, she had waited for the world around her to change. And it had.

Just by existing as a woman in power Merkel changed German society and the world.

DARE TO BE THE ONLY
WOMAN IN THE ROOM

From the time she entered university throughout her earliest years as a politician, Merkel found herself surrounded by men. She was often the only young woman in her physics and chemistry classes at Leipzig University and throughout her time at the Academy of Sciences; the only other women worked on the administrative side. Whether because of this, or her commonsense approach to life, Merkel always seemed to struggle to see herself as extraordinary. Once she decided that she wanted power, she understood how to get it and keep it. But Merkel never spent much time dwelling on the idea that what she was doing or achieved might be unique or extraordinary.

As far as she was concerned, she wasn't doing anything different from those around her. "Parity in all areas just seems logical to me," Merkel said when asked about her relationship to feminism and whether she focused on promoting women. "It's not something I have to constantly bring up."[9]

But she found subtle ways to make her point. In the "family photos" taken at the annual gatherings of the leaders of the world's leading developed economies—the United States, Britain, Canada, France, Germany, Italy, and Japan—Merkel would always appear in her brightest shades of pale peach, ruby-red, or robin's-egg-blue blazers. Flanked on either side by suits in various shades of black, navy, or charcoal, she knew that she would be easy to spot. Her presence, as a woman, in the ranks of the world's most powerful leaders could not be missed.

In much the same way that the Obamas during their years in the

White House brought African American, Native American, and Latin artists and performers there to shine a light on their culture, Merkel as a trained scientist and a power-hungry politician highlighted for Germans the role that women can play in society, beyond jobs in the care sector. Merkel may not have talked feminism, but through her longevity and the respect that she earned in her sixteen years in office, she lived it.

Occasionally, she would even acknowledge the hole she had bashed into the glass ceiling and the impact that her chancellorship might have made in the lives of the girls and women who would follow in her political footsteps. During a visit to Tel Aviv in 2018, at a meeting of business leaders, Merkel found herself seated at a U-shaped table beside Prime Minister Benjamin Netanyahu and twenty-five Israeli tech and business executives, all more or less like him. Glancing around the room at the sea of dark suits, Merkel bluntly remarked, "It would be nice if next time some women were present. This seems to still be a very male domain."[10] Mr. Netanyahu snapped, "You're right." But the chancellor's comment caused an uproar among leading women in Israel's tech industry. In response, they printed a life-size cutout of Merkel and posed alongside it, flanked by some of their male colleagues and a few children, for an alternative photo that made the rounds on social media, making sure that their own government saw what they felt Merkel had understood. Their message, inspired by Merkel, was clear: competent women leaders could be found throughout the industry; they simply hadn't been invited.

Drawing on the dry humor that she normally kept tightly under wraps while in public, Merkel acknowledged understanding the power she could provide as a role model, telling an audience of young leaders in 2018 that maybe for girls she could serve as a role model that a woman could survive in this space. Even survive very well.[11]

Merkel had learned early on how to survive in spaces where others might not think she belonged. Whether it was standing up to the man considered the most powerful in the world, who belittled not only her person, but her country and her decisions, or sitting as the only woman flanked by the leaders of the world's leading industrial countries, Merkel acted as though there was no difference between her and those around her. She simply demonstrated that her power was equal to theirs and refused to let herself be defined by her gender.

IGNORE IMPOSTOR SYNDROME
AND MAKE YOURSELF USEFUL

In 1991, when putting together his new cabinet, the first of reunified Germany, Chancellor Helmut Kohl needed to have enough ministers from the former GDR. The women in his party had also been pushing for more representation, so he realized he could not fill his ministries only with men. But there were a lot of men looking for posts, including those who might be owed a political favor. He needed every post he could get. Enter Angela Merkel. By naming her, a woman from the former East Germany, as his minister for women and youth, he filled two minority requirements with one individual. Merkel remained clear-eyed about how she landed a position in government, with little real experience in politics and no network to back her. Not worrying that she had only been given the position because of her gender and GDR background, Merkel didn't become paralyzed by impostor syndrome and instead seized the opportunity presented to her. She read everything she could, consulted with the people whom she had met and felt she could trust, and formed a team around her that helped her to navigate the ins and outs of a political system that was, at the time, still quite foreign to her. She had learned from her entry into the political system that it could pay to be useful. "I was young, a woman, and came from the East," she acknowledged years later, when offering advice to a young woman about how to get involved in politics. "There were a lot of uses for me."[12]

Upon assuming the position of minister for women and youth, one of the first projects that she took on was to draw up the Gender Equality Act.

She had her ministry carry out a study to support the effort to pass a law that would make sexual harassment a crime. Her ministry found that 72 percent of the 778 women queried had been targets of sexual harassment while on the job. But those who complained risked losing their job—that happened in forty-six out of fifty cases. Only in three instances were the men fired.[13]

Two years later, the young minister agreed to write a critique of Susan Faludi's *Backlash* in Germany's leading feminist magazine, *Emma* (whose publisher, Alice Schwarzer, one of Germany's leading feminists, Merkel would befriend). Merkel's essay, from 1993, read as a rallying cry for women in Germany to take up the mantle of power and use it to bring about change. "As long as [women] are not represented in the leading positions of the media, political parties, interest groups, business and social sectors; as long as they are not among the fashion designers and top chefs, guidelines will simply be set by men for an equally long time," she wrote, daring to sound more feminist than she ever did once she had been elected chancellor. She said that the lesson she had drawn from Faludi's book had been to keep pushing the boundaries of what society allowed. "We women must go further on the march through the institutions and participate in public power."[14]

At the start of her career, many found it easy to write off Merkel as an exception brought in to fill a quota. But she legitimized herself and rose above attempts to question her right to be in the room where it happens by refusing to dwell on how she came to power. Instead she focused on learning everything she could about the positions she held and using the knowledge she acquired to bring about the change she believed was needed.

LET YOUR ACTIONS
SPEAK FOR YOUR BELIEFS

Three years into Donald Trump's presidency, Merkel had experienced the forty-fifth U.S. president enough to understand whom she was dealing with. He had taunted her over social media and pointedly refused to shake her hand. But worse in her eyes he was weakening the democratic and multilateral structures that had helped secure Germany's position as a peaceful, economically powerful nation in a prospering Europe. For years, she had brushed off the president's slights and asides, seeming to embrace Michelle Obama's idea of "when they go low, we go high."

Merkel embraced Germany's government policy of not commenting on internal affairs in other countries. But when she was asked during a news conference in July 2019 whether she supported the U.S. congresswomen of color whom Trump had baited by telling the four—Representatives Ilhan Omar of Minnesota, Alexandria Ocasio-Cortez of New York, Ayanna S. Pressley of Massachusetts, and Rashida Tlaib of Michigan—to return to their own countries, Merkel replied with a firm, clipped, "Ja."

In any other circumstance, such an expression of solidarity might have gone largely unnoticed. But with the world in an uproar over a U.S. president who had used vulgar language to refer to women and seemed intent on rolling back rights that had been fought for and won over decades, Merkel sensed the importance of the moment. She said that she "feels solidarity" with the Democratic lawmakers, known as the Squad.[15] It was a rare moment for the chancellor to step out of her normal restraint and drive home a point that she did not always choose to make, but those of us who had watched her long enough understood. Merkel might not shout her feminism from the rooftops, but in the background she encouraged women at every chance she could. Some of the most obvious ways were to directly empower peers, such as Ursula von der Leyen, who would in 2019 go on to become the first woman appointed president of the European Commission, the highest official in the European Union. Merkel's two most important advisers were women—leading to snarky remarks about her "girls' camp" in the chancellery. By her fourth term in office, she had achieved gender parity in her staff.

At cabinet meetings, she also made sure that every one of her ministers received equal time to speak, regardless of their seniority or gender. Starting in April 2006, Merkel invited girls and young women to the chancellery every year to kick off the nationwide Girls' Day event, aimed at encouraging more young women to consider jobs and research in science. When she was awarded Finland's first International Gender Equality Prize in 2017, she donated the entire 150,000-euro award to a shelter dedicated to protecting women from violence in the West African country of Niger. Typical of Merkel, she made no large announcement about the donation, instead letting the gesture speak for itself. In an age of self-promoters, when people seem eager to broadcast even their smallest accomplishments, Merkel often instead chose understatement. But when the moment demanded it, she opted to use her position and ultimately her voice to make it clear that she believed women's rights are human rights, and all people should be treated equal, regardless of their gender or beliefs.

SOME GENDERS ARE
MORE EQUAL THAN OTHERS

Although women made up a significant part of the workforce on the shop floors and in the fields of East Germany, they were markedly absent from positions of leadership or power both in politics and business. Despite the claims of equality in the Communist nation and the benefits that women enjoyed, the decisions about which jobs they could carry out, how many hours they could work, and how long they could remain at home after the birth of a child were not decided by the East German women. None of the full members of the Politburo, the executive body of the former East Germany's ruling Communist Party government, were women. When two women made it into the committee, they were not granted voting rights, rendering their presence equivalent to decoration, or window-dressing equality. The positions of leadership in the large state-owned companies also remained dominated by men. Despite the rhetoric that men and women were equal comrades, "It was men who were sitting in the places where important decisions were made."[16]

Even the daily workload reflected this imbalance. Women put in an equal number of hours in the fields or on the factory floors as their male counterparts, but while the men could go home to their evening beer after a day's work, women began their second shift. Women got the children ready in the mornings and out the door to day care or schools, before heading off to their day jobs, which often began at 6:00 or 6:30 a.m.[17] Women oversaw homework, prepared dinner, and brought the children to bed. In between, women did the shopping—often an exercise in futility that meant running from one store to the next or standing in seemingly endless lines to secure even basic goods, which often remained scarce in East Germany. For all the laws that guaranteed women and men equal pay and equal access to opportunity, women earned roughly 30 percent less than their male counterparts.[18]

For role models and inspiration during her youth, Merkel looked abroad to France. One of the women she admired was Marie Curie, the Polish-born French physicist and chemist who became one of the first women to study at the Sorbonne and later became the first woman professor at the university. In 1903, she became the first woman to win a Nobel Prize, for her research in physics, and won a second Nobel in chemistry, eight years later. Merkel also immersed herself in the writings of Simone de Beauvoir, the French intellectual and writer whose seminal analysis on the oppression of women, *The Second Sex*, helped lay the foundations for modern feminist theory. Yet Merkel claimed later it was not de Beauvoir's arguments about feminism that drew her to the Frenchwoman's writings.

"In Simone de Beauvoir I saw much more a strong woman who came from the middle class, who succeeded in just making her own path," she said, adding that Curie's achievement at breaking through in the scientific world was equally inspiring.[19] "These women impressed me."

After reunification, women from the former East were praised for their competencies and the natural ease with which they combined their home life with their jobs. But many were shocked at the standards they met on the other side of the former border, where women from the West had been raised to believe that they had to choose between children or a career. Those who dared to take on both were shamed as *Rabbenmütter*, or "raven mothers," women who leave their children alone in the nest to fly away to their careers. This outdated and uniquely German insult prevailed for decades, effectively guilting women into choosing between a career and having children. As recently as the early 2000s, when I arrived in Germany, it was rare to find other working mothers among the press corps, or in Germany's leading companies. Those mothers who did work were often in lower-paying jobs or worked part-time, so they could compensate for the lack of sufficient childcare. In Merkel's sixteen years in power, that changed. Her governments shifted policies to expand childcare and ensure that schools provided either lessons or after-school care into the afternoons, making it not only possible but increasingly socially acceptable for young women—and men—to balance jobs and raising a family. Merkel took what she witnessed as lip service to gender equality in East Germany and made it a reality.

The change brought Germany's family-leave policy more in line with the Scandinavian countries that Germany is often compared to in the minds of many Americans. Unlike in the United States, where childcare is viewed as the parents' responsibility and paid leave to care for a sick family member is rare, the changes that Merkel's first government enacted set the tone for a shift toward accepting that women were a valuable resource not only as mothers but as members of the workforce.

LOOKS AREN'T EVERYTHING, BUT THEY CAN BE USEFUL

Merkel's understanding of power is deeply entwined with her intellect and instinct, her ability to absorb information and use it. She often appeared more annoyed than interested in the public attention and media spotlight that are trained on the chancellor, blowing off the opportunity to sit for a portrait by Annie Leibovitz, the star photographer renowned for her images of powerful women from Hillary Clinton to Taylor Swift, when *Vogue* ran a profile of Merkel in 2017. But as she rose through the ranks of political power, from minister to party leader, to head of the opposition and ultimately the chancellery, Merkel realized that while she might consider her appearance secondary to the ministers she chose or the laws she proposed, the world around her did not. If she wanted to maintain power, she had to look the part. Unlike the men around her, that meant more than just which color and cut of suit she wore. "Who Wants to Lead Must Be Beautiful," read the headline in a leading German weekly that summarized Merkel's evolution from her bowl-cut days to her discovery of a stylist before her first campaign for the chancellery.[20] Merkel wanted to lead.

Sabine Bergmann-Pohl, like Merkel, hailed from the former East Germany. She had served as that country's last head of state. Later she found herself alongside Merkel in reunited Germany's first government. She was shocked at what she saw.

"When she was new in politics, she had a terrible haircut," Bergmann-Pohl recalled. "She came back from an interview, and she was a little bit made up. I said to her, 'Angela, you look so nice, people don't just listen to what you say, they look at how you look. Just dress up a little nicely and you'll see, it's all much easier.'"

To Merkel, the close-clipped hairstyle that everyone around her called a bowl cut was practical and easy to manage. To her peers and the wider public, it was the butt of constant jokes. "Helmut Kohl's hairstyle—if that's what you would call what he has atop his head—has never been an issue," wrote one of Merkel's earliest biographers, reflecting on the thin gray strands that Chancellor Kohl had worn brushed back from his deeply receding hairline. "But with Angela Merkel it never ceases to be a national issue. In every newspaper, at every party, there were jokes about Angela Merkel's hairstyle and serious debates about whether it was a Prince Valiant or Joan of Arc hairstyle."[21]

A decade later, Berlin had replaced Bonn as the German capital and Merkel had dethroned Kohl and risen through the ranks to become the leader of the conservative Christian Democratic Union, the main opposition party in the German parliament at the time. By then she had taken her former colleague's remark to heart and swapped the hippie-length skirts, buttoned-up blouses, and hand-knit cardigans for more business-like attire, mostly dark pantsuits. But her hairstyle remained practical. Now worn as a straight jaw-length bob with heavy bangs that fell just above her eyes, it remained fair game.

In 2001, Sixt, one of Germany's leading rental-car agencies, published an ad featuring two black-and-white portraits of Merkel, one alongside the other. In the image on the left, her hair hung down in its usual flat bob, tucked behind her ears. Beneath it a caption read, "Want a new hairstyle?" The right-hand photo showed the same image of Merkel's face, but her heavy bob had been photoshopped to appear blown off the crown of her head, effectively standing on end, as if she had been caught in a windstorm or a high-speed joyride. Beneath it, the caption read, "Rent a convertible."[22] The ad was everywhere, and everyone was talking about it. When a reporter asked Merkel what she thought about seeing herself made fun of nearly everywhere in print, on television, and on billboards, across the country, Merkel coolly replied, "That is an interesting style suggestion."[23] While her hairstyle may not have changed radically, what had was Merkel's understanding of the rules of the game.

Ever the student, Merkel listened to the criticism, but instead of caving to it, she found her own pragmatist way to use it to her advantage. As discussion about the image persisted, she used the situation to push her political agenda. She wrote a letter to the head of the car rental company and saw to it that a copy fell into the hands of Germany's widest-read newspaper, *Bild*. "I have noticed your company mainly because of your cars," the letter read. "But that it can also be quite hairy to become your customer, I only now understood from your advertising." However, Sixt "unfortunately made a mistake," she said. Merkel, who was leader of the opposition in parliament, explained that her hair wasn't standing on end because she rode in a convertible, but because she had read the government's proposed tax law.[24] It was classic Merkel, not only refusing to bend to criticism of her appearance but getting the better of the joke by using it as yet another tool for leadership.

USING STYLE TO SEND A MESSAGE?

By the time she launched her campaign for the chancellery in 2005, Merkel had understood it was time for a new look. She approached the man known as Berlin's stylist of the stars and tasked him with coming up with a cut for a *Kanzlerin*—a woman chancellor. "Before she came to me, her hairstyle was called a bowl cut," Udo Walz, the stylist, conceded.[25] He got to work, shortening the length at the back, adding volume and highlights to soften and brighten her appearance. Once she became chancellor, Merkel hired a professional stylist to join her team. Starting every morning by having her makeup done became part of her routine.

But makeup and a new hairstyle only solved part of her problem. She still had to decide what to wear. Long gone were the flowing skirts and hand-knit cardigans, replaced by standard women's pantsuits. Even back when she had the time, Merkel had never been much of a shopper. What she wanted was a system, a look that would be uncomplicated, while still allowing her to express herself. Above all, she wanted a look that was so predictable, it would not attract any more attention than the suits and ties her male counterparts wore. It was her husband who pointed out that a fellow lawmaker's brightly colored blazers always looked smart and suggested that such a look might suit her well.

Without knowing it he had inspired a style celebrated by fans on Instagram as #merkellooks, for its combination of utter predictability—

blazer with three or four buttons and pockets in various cuts over straight black pants and flat shoes—with an ever-changing palette of colors that added a touch of fun. What brooches were for Madeleine Albright, the hundreds of pins that she donned to transmit messages during her years in public service, blazers were for Merkel. Those of us who watched her closely would often swap speculations over which mood was reflected in pale peach or bright lilac. Black blazers were reserved for more serious or somber occasions, shades of her favorite color, blue, for when she was happy or wanted to transmit calm. Green was supposed to signal optimism, but it backfired when she arrived in Athens in 2012 wearing the same pale green blazer she had worn the night that Germany beat Greece in that year's European soccer championship, a match that had pitted the deeply indebted Greeks against their largest creditor.

Only once, during her first term in office, did Merkel dare to deviate from the look that had become her professional uniform. In 2008, she attended the gala inauguration of Norway's new state opera house in Oslo wearing a full-length gown with a plunging neckline framed by a petrol-colored velvet stole. Her décolleté made headlines around Europe that weekend, winning praise from the French and Italians, who commended her for "sparkling," but shocking the Turks and much of her own public at home. "Deep Merkel," exclaimed *Günes*, a daily newspaper in Turkey, while Germany's *Die Welt* contemplated, "How much décolleté should a chancellor show?"

Questions about Merkel's daring dress dominated the routine government news conference the following Monday. Where he would normally announce policy and travel plans and field journalists' questions on an array of topics from pension reform to the government's position on world conflicts, Merkel's seasoned deputy spokesman, Thomas Steg, struggled to keep a straight face as he found himself forced to comment on his boss's fashion choice.

"The chancellor has been a bit taken aback," he said. "The fact that this evening gown, a new composition, a new arrangement from the chancellor's closet, has caused such a furor was not the chancellor's intention."[26]

Several days later, in an interview on public TV, Merkel herself put an end to the discussion by pointing out how gendered it was. If a man occupied the chancellery, then nobody would be worried about what he wore. "It's simply because in Germany a woman is chancellor," she said.[27]

But Merkel learned from the experience. Never again would she appear in public wearing any article of clothing that could cause such a stir. Or so she thought. Six years later, Merkel's dress made headlines again, this time not for its cut, but for its reappearance. The chancellor, one year into her third term in office, sent the German and British press into a frenzy when she appeared at the annual Salzburg music festival wrapped in a pink, black, yellow, and turquoise print tunic over a long black skirt. This time, her dress revealed not her plunging neckline, but her penchant for recycled fashion. Pictures from cultural events that she attended more than a decade earlier showed her wearing the exact same item of clothing. "Angela Merkel's Been Wearing the Same Amazing Tunic for 18 Years," read the headline in a story that appeared in the online magazine *Slate*, reflecting on the chancellor's fashion choice and citing the German press as praising Merkel for "remaining true to herself."[28] Because this fashion uproar took place around the time when Michelle Obama was being praised for repeatedly wearing the same dress to Easter Sunday services one year and again for a reception for the former president Bush Sr., Merkel received more praise than outrage for her repeat wearing. Nevertheless, she was once again reminded how quickly public attention could deviate from demanding answers about her position on matters of state to commenting on the origin of her tunic dress, a favorite piece, purchased on one of her first trips to California, which had made multiple appearances at opera festivals over the years.

Keen observers were not surprised. Merkel's practical bend, disdain for shopping, and lack of time meant that she had been recycling fashion

long before it was a buzzword in an industry obsessed with its endless
cycle of new collections. She chose a professional tailor, who had trained
in New York City, to design her array of blazers, altering only their color
and the material—often imported from Italy—but rarely their cut. And
her California tunic was not the only favorite piece to put in repeat appearances at opera festivals; she returned to the Salzburg classical music
festival in a silk jacket in pale lilac over a long skirt in 2010, three years
after wearing the outfit the first time. She appeared in an off-the-shoulder
gown in deep turquoise at the annual festival of Richard Wagner's operas
in 2008 and again in 2012—in 2007, she wore the lilac ensemble.

By that time, Merkel had grown confident enough to understand that
clothes could be used to transmit a message. By choosing to shop for her
own dresses instead of borrowing couture from selected designers and
not shying away from re-wearing her old favorites, Merkel sent the message that practicality and modesty remained at the core of her identity.
"My outfit is very straightforward," she said, in discussing her choice of
dress. "And very German."[29]

Unlike a First Lady, whose job does not come with clearly defined
goals, making her fashion into a way to show off personality and
purposely promote designers, Merkel's job was to govern a country
that was the world's third-largest economy and the de facto leader of
Europe. Clothes had to serve her needs, not the other way around. In
fact, she actively sought to downplay the importance of her fashion
choices, revealing in the last months of her chancellorship that when
she believed it time to take one of her brightly colored blazers out of
her wardrobe rotation, it landed in the clothing recycling bin. Representatives from the charitable organization Oxfam, seeing an opportunity, approached the chancellor and suggested that she select a couple
of the blazers that they could auction off, raising proceeds for a charity
of her choice. The chancellor quietly declined.[30] Her blazers should
not be handled any differently from anyone else's. She also made clear
that "none of my clothes are going to a museum."[31]

Merkel never selected specific fashion designers for her wardrobe but nevertheless understood that she could communicate through her clothes. It wasn't through shining a light on a particular representative of a group or a cause that she sought to elevate, but a way of life. She had come from a country where designing your own clothes was a political statement—in a world where even fashion was dictated by the government, such deviance made clear where you stood politically. But by choosing instead to focus on the ability to reuse and recycle favorite pieces, she sent the message that sustainability was not just a buzzword for her, but a way of life.

Madame Tussauds Berlin, the waxworks museum, may not have heeded the chancellor's admonishment to keep her clothes out of a museum, but they did hear the message she sought to send with them loud and clear. In the final days of her chancellorship, they dressed their model of Merkel in the chancellor's best-known recycled fashion look: her summer-holiday hiking outfit. Year after year, photos of Merkel dressed in the same red-checked shirt, thick-soled hiking boots, pants with side pockets in a quick-drying fabric, and a cap, pulled firmly down to the arch of her eyebrows, would find their way onto the front pages. Always keen to take a jab at the Germans, the British tabloids sought to sensationalize the chancellor's down-to-earth approach to her vacation attire in 2017, ahead of her final campaign for the chancellery.

"Merkel is pictured on a hiking trip wearing the same holiday outfit in the same location for the FIFTH year running," read a headline in Britain's *Daily Mail,* splashed above a series of photos taken in successive years, showing the chancellor wearing the exact same plaid shirt over the same light-colored pants.[32] Undeterred—or perhaps inspired—by the failed uproar, Merkel wore the same gear again the following year. Merkel never let critics affect her choice of clothing, which is just one of the many bold statements she made with her appearance.

By the time she left office, Merkel had succeeded in downplaying her dressing to the point that it failed to draw attention in her day-to-day affairs. At the same time, she had developed a look all her own and immediately recognizable. Anna Wintour, the long-standing editor of *Vogue* who is widely considered the defining voice in the world of fashion, agreed. She praised Merkel's look as "very authentic" and immediately associated with the chancellor's persona. "She looks like Angela Merkel. I'm glad she has this recognizable style; she looks to me like someone who knows who she is."[33]

NEUTRALIZING *MUTTI*

Toward the end of her first term in office, the chancellor was suddenly being referred to as *Mutti*, or "mom." The term was born out of the 2008 global financial downturn, when Merkel drew on a character well-known to Germans, the *schwäbische Hausfrau*, the housewife from the southwestern region of Swabia, as the embodiment of thrift. The character was reputed to keep her home and family running on modest means, by scrimping and saving, and could serve as an example of how Europe could find a way out of the crisis.

"It is actually quite simple. All we had to do was ask a Swabian housewife," Merkel said. "She would have given us a short but true piece of wisdom, which is, you cannot live beyond your means in the long run. That is the core of the crisis."[34]

The maxim of the Swabian housewife became a mantra that Merkel repeated time and again over the next few years, as European leaders wrangled over a way out of the debt crisis, eventually agreeing on a fiscal treaty that ensured Greece and other indebted countries remained in the group of countries that use the common European currency, the euro. But the price was bitter and high. The mantra of the Swabian housewife came to be synonymous with the preachy tone of an overbearing mother, which is how Merkel was viewed in many European capitals and by an increasing number of Germans who feared she was putting their hard-earned money at risk.

Yet years later in 2015, the moniker took on a different meaning when Merkel refused to close her country's borders to tens of thousands of people, most of them fleeing conflict in the Middle East or Afghanistan. Sudden she became Mutter Angela, as featured on the cover of the German weekly *Der Spiegel*, clad in a white habit with blue stripes, in reference to that worn by Mother Teresa.[35] As more and more people arrived in their country, a growing number of Germans became increasingly angry at what they saw as newcomers who were benefiting from the generous social welfare system without contributing to it. (In fact, many migrants wanted to begin working immediately, but were prevented from doing so by German law.) As protests spread across the country, people shouted slurs at the chancellor and demanded that *"Mutti Merkel"* had to go.

At the same time, many of the roughly 1 million people who arrived in Germany from 2015 to 2016 seeking asylum from the wars in their home countries, mostly Syria, held and expressed deep gratitude to the chancellor for refusing to close her country's borders. Along with Germans who respected the chancellor for showing courage and humanity with her decision to allow so many people in, they revived the nickname "Mutti." But they meant it as a term of affection and respect. Running with that idea, Merkel's party took ownership of the nickname, weaving it into their campaign slogans. When she ran for her fourth and final term in office, supporters brandished posters and T-shirts that read FULLY *mutti*-VATED.

Once again, Merkel had outfoxed her critics, taking an idea they had used to undermine her and turning it around to highlight her strengths. Instead of allowing *Mutti* as an insult or disparagement of her abilities, she flipped it on its head, drawing on the positive associations that many have with mothers, as a force of competent stability. By the time she was entering into her final four years in office, *Mutti* had become a term of endearment, a reflection of Merkel's ability, throughout her leadership, to create the impression that she was in charge, so others needn't worry. Even when political infighting seemed to engulf her government, or strains among Germany's European partners appeared poised to threaten the unity of the bloc, Merkel engendered trust by remaining calm and searching for a solution.

Although Merkel never overtly sought to play her gender, by drawing on her experiences of growing up in a society where women were considered equal in the workforce and by refusing to bow to stereotypes of how she should look or lead, Merkel succeeded in redefining female power. By the time she left office, Mutti Merkel had transformed the *Vaterland*, the fatherland, bringing reunited Germany into the twenty-first century, as the mother of the nation.

Chapter 2

THE ART OF WAITING

She is not only incompetent,
politically she is profusely naïve.
—GERHARD SCHRÖDER, 1996

The night that Angela Merkel won the chancellery, nobody in Germany seemed ready to believe it. She did. Sitting under the glaring lights of a TV studio hours after her party's narrow victory over the incumbent chancellor had been announced, a sly smile played across her lips as the reality dawned for her. On the other side of the studio, the sitting chancellor, her rival Gerhard Schröder, had spread out the full fan of his machismo like a peacock in a mating dance. But he was not trying to attract the attention of the woman seated across from him. Quite the opposite.

"Do you seriously believe that my party would accept an offer of talks from Ms. Merkel in this situation? Saying that she would like to become chancellor? I mean, I think we have to leave the church in the village,"[1] Schröder puffed, uttering a phrase that Germans use when they mean "let's not get carried away here."

But the soon-to-be-former chancellor wasn't finished. He spelled out the possible political tie-ups that presented themselves after the results showed his center-left Social Democratic Party only three seats behind Merkel's conservative Christian Democratic Union (after a delayed vote

in one district, the lead held by Merkel's party would grow to four seats).
Up until that very moment, Germany's unwritten political norms and
traditions dictated that it fell to Merkel as the leader of the party with the
most votes to try to build a government. The most obvious option was to
find a way to get the defeated chancellor's party on board. Now here was
Schröder publicly talking down that option.

"She will not manage a coalition under her leadership with my Social
Democratic Party," he blustered, raising questions among others on the
stage about what he had been up to before taking his seat. "That is clear.
Don't kid yourself about that."

If there had been any doubt in Angela Merkel's mind until that point
that she would become Germany's next chancellor, it evaporated in that
moment. She said nothing, but returned his gaze with a barely visible but
confidently triumphant smile.

When the moderators turned to her to seek a response, she answered
with the even, straightforward tone of voice that would come to define
Germany to the world for the next sixteen years. Merkel laid out the facts
as she saw them. It was up to her and her party to "build a sensible subsequent government out of the result that voters have delivered," she said.

Then, turning to her rival as would a teacher lecturing a naughty
schoolboy, she raised her left hand to emphasize her point: "It is plain
and simple that you did not win tonight." She looked him in the eye as
he puffed and postured in his seat. "That is the reality."

Ask any woman who has been alone in a room full of men. (A situation that for Merkel had been the norm from the time she started studying physics as a young woman at Leipzig University up through her days
as a researcher at the Academy of Sciences.) When faced with attempts to
belittle your point of view or put you down simply because of your gender, you don't have many options. You can either ignore them and stand
your ground, or you can fire back and find a way to put them down.

Few people watching that night realized they were witnessing a dis-
play of one of Merkel's great abilities, the art of biding her time, allow-

ing opponents to bluster and fume, while calmly sizing up the situation before responding with the unflappable accuracy (on more than one occasion to devastating effect) to disarm whoever appeared to stand in her way or question her authority. Merkel's patience in the face of a problem was often mistaken for indecision, not a unique capacity to remain calm and wait for the right moment to make her move. Her years working as a research scientist had taught her the merits of exploring and weighing all sides of an option, a process that she knew could not be rushed. Deliberation and reflection before action were defining principles of her nature and would come to define her chancellorship.

THINK BEFORE JUMPING

Angela Merkel was a schoolgirl when she first began to understand her need to think things over before she should act. At the time, it may not have appeared to her as a particularly beneficial trait. But by the time she had decided to seek a fourth and final term in office, after more than a decade in power, she knew herself and how she approached a problem.

For years, she would recount an anecdote from her childhood to journalists and anyone else seeking to understand and explain her thought process. To this day, elementary school children in Germany are taught how to swim as part of their physical education classes. Merkel, just a child at the time, had been no exception. At age nine she was faced with a test that required she jump from a ten-foot-high diving board. She climbed the ladder and stepped carefully down the length of the plank, staring alternately into the water below and at the teacher waiting to grade her for making the leap.

A clock on the wall ticked down the minutes of the hour-long class. Merkel knew that she had to jump before it ended or earn a failing mark. Her options were few and obvious—jump or retreat. Still, she stood motionless, turning them over in her head for three-quarters of an hour.

Not until the sharp cry of the teacher's whistle signaled that time was up did Merkel plunge into the pool. She had used the time allotted and left everyone around her questioning whether she would move, but when the time came, she moved.

By the end of her chancellery, the tale had been told so often it had worn thin. Yet it gave clarity to anyone, including critics, baffled by what appeared to be an inability to make up her mind or act. Yet its accuracy remained unfailingly true, as became obvious in late 2016 when the world wondered whether Merkel would seek a fourth term as chancellor.

Throughout the summer of 2016, she had bided her time, insisting that she would make up her mind when the time was right. But when was that? Years before her first election, Merkel had vowed that she would leave power on her own terms. "At some point I would like to find the right time to leave politics," she said in 1998. "I don't want to be a half-dead wreck."[2] We all wondered, after three terms in office and the upheavals and political backlash at home and in Europe that surrounded her decision to allow a million migrants into the country, had Merkel finally had enough? The chancellor gave us no clues.

Then came the election of Donald Trump as forty-fifth president of the United States. As the vote drew closer, Germans had repeatedly asked me, with a mix of curiosity and disbelief, whether I thought he even stood a chance of defeating Hillary Clinton. When he did, it quickly became obvious that Merkel, along with her entire government, had failed to prepare for that possibility. No one had ever made a serious effort to reach out to the Trump campaign, and they found themselves caught completely off guard.

Days later, President Obama, now a lame duck, arrived in Berlin for a farewell tour that included a dinner between the two leaders. Much has been made about the pressure Obama is said to have put on the German leader to remain in power because he saw her as a stabilizing force to ensure the continuation of Western democracy. Seeing the United States headed for a period of nationalist populism caused alarm in Germany, where many saw parallels to their own country in the 1930s, when Adolf Hitler rose to power. But Merkel's aides said she had been equally concerned about the state of affairs at home, with the backlash growing against her immigration policy and frustration building with a lack of innovation, despite her three terms talking about the need for a transformation to green energy. It was a difficult decision, but Merkel knew she had no obvious successor, and she had pledged at the outset of her pursuit of the chancellery in 2005 to serve her party and her country.

After weeks of weighing her options and discussions with her closest confidants, including her husband, Merkel took the podium at her party's headquarters on November 20 and recalled that pledge, adding that many people had made clear to her they thought it would be irresponsible if she chose not to run again. When a reporter asked her whether Obama had played a role in her decision, Merkel effectively returned to the diving-board scenario. Aware that eleven years into her chancellorship her response described more than the most recent decision being discussed, she didn't answer the question directly; instead she said, "I need a long time and the decisions come late—but then I stand by them."[3]

KEEP YOUR EYES
OPEN FOR OPPORTUNITIES

The day that it became clear that Merkel would become the first woman, the first person from the former East Germany, and the first to be born after World War II to serve as German chancellor, journalists packed her party's headquarters. For weeks, Merkel had been in discussions with her rival's party to hammer out an agreement as the road map for her future government. Heading into those talks, a tradition carried out by all political parties in Germany that find themselves needing to work together with a partner to secure a majority in parliament that can allow them to govern, she had taken the approach of waiting, as she had said, for things to "sort themselves out." By that, she meant returning to the negotiating table time and again, until her erstwhile rival, Schröder, agreed to step aside, allowing a new government to form. This time, one led by Merkel as the chancellor.

Every journalist in Berlin had packed the party headquarters, waiting for the future chancellor to take the podium to answer their burning questions about her plans for tax reform, who would populate her cabinet, and how much would be spent promoting research. Germany was facing a historic moment, and all anyone was asking about were the details of domestic politics. It was Judy Dempsey, then correspondent for the *International Herald Tribune*, who swooped in to save the day, asking the question burning in the minds of those of us who observed Germany for the world beyond its borders. Our readers cared less about who would get which ministry and whether Merkel planned to raise taxes and by how much. A woman taking power in one of the world's leading industrial powers for the first time—a feat that at that time and still nearly two decades later remains unachieved in the United States and unimaginable to large swaths of American society—was the story of the day. "Mrs. Merkel, you will be the first woman chancellor of Germany—how are you? Are you happy?"[4]

Laughter broke out among the German correspondents, as Merkel paused to think over her answer. For a moment, it looked as if she was confronted for the first time with the magnitude of her achievement. Then, her face lit up with a smile and Merkel beamed. "I'm doing well." Then, as swiftly as it had appeared, her smile faded, as if she was catching herself under the weight of the office she would now assume. Abruptly, she switched back into business mode. "I think we have a lot of work ahead of us."[5]

After spending the initial years of her career in a lab studying slides under a microscope and figuring complex chemistry calculations, Merkel entered politics with no idea about the workings—or even the positions—of the political parties vying for her support. In the months after the Berlin Wall came down, parties from West Germany began canvassing for new members in the East, where other grassroots organizations were springing up on their own. Sensing that she wanted to get involved, but with no realization of how profoundly politics would alter her life, Merkel and a colleague attended various events, checking out their tones and messages to find the right fit. Many East Germans, including Merkel's mother, joined the Social Democratic Party, which traced its roots to the workers' movement in the late nineteenth century. But Merkel didn't like that everyone in the SDP called one another "comrade" and was immediately on a first-name basis—a level of intimacy that to this day many, especially older Germans, still withhold from their acquaintances and colleagues even after years of working together. The tradition signals a level of professionalism and respect, and throughout her time in office, Merkel made the point of only ever addressing her closest aide by her surname—at least when they were together in public.

The party that eventually caught Merkel's attention was the Demokratischer Aufbruch, or Democratic Awakening, a party founded by reform-minded East Germans with their own vision for democracy in their country. Like Merkel, many of its members belonged to the Lutheran Church, which had long supported dissidents in the former East, helping to organize the protests in 1989 and shelter demonstrators when the police moved in. But after Germany held its first joint elections, aimed at swiftly solidifying reunification, the party was absorbed by West Germany's dominant conservative force, the Christian Democratic Union. The move left many of its members disappointed, but not Angela Merkel. She had admired the conservative party's leader, Chancellor Helmut Kohl, for the speed with which he had moved to ensure that East Germany ceased to exist, absorbed like the protest party she had joined into the greater whole of a reunited Germany. She made sure that she was introduced to the chancellor. Months later, he responded by selecting her to serve as a minister in his government and as a political protégé.

One of Merkel's greatest criticisms of the Communist-run system in East Germany was that it failed to support its citizens. Under the strict regime, more concerned with creating jobs for everyone than for seeing that the best people were in those positions, individuals had been prevented from testing their own limits. For a mind such as Merkel's, such intellectual confinement had been tantamount to a crime. Asked in 1998 what she considered to be the best part of her life as a politician then, Merkel looked back. Reflecting on the limitations that had been imposed on her during the first three decades of her life under Communist rule, she named the opportunity to discover a talent she had been unaware she possessed. "Reaching my performance limits in an area where I see my strength; creative collaboration with people," she said. "In East Germany, we were never challenged."[6]

It was Merkel's quest for a new challenge that had lured her away from the confines of the chemistry lab when she first walked into the offices of the Democratic Awakening. There, in a corner of the makeshift office where the party would meet, Merkel found boxes sent from West Germany. Opening them, she found they held computers, at the time already a standard tool for any administrative work in the West, but in the former East Germany still relatively rare. In her years as a scientist in her country's leading research academy, Merkel had worked with more primitive versions of what had arrived. The machines in the boxes may have been more sophisticated than what top scientists from the East could access, but they worked on the same basic principles. But nobody else among the many intellectuals and politicians seemed to know what to do with the donation. Merkel began unpacking the computers, plugging them in, and explaining to the others how they worked. She sensed that her home country was at a turning point, that she and others like her who were unafraid of seizing change and throwing themselves into the unknown could be a part of shaping a new future. For once, she didn't hesitate because she knew exactly what to do: embrace the chance to prove herself.

"We could lend a hand, we could roll up our sleeves, ultimately to be a part of the negotiations for German unity. Those were incredible days, weeks, and months," she recalled two decades later. "Not asking what can't, but what can be done."[7]

This guiding force, to search for opportunities to be useful, carried Merkel, like a wave, to the highest level of political power. She rode it from her earliest days in politics, viewing the uncertainty as a chance to try new things and push her limits. That is how she earned her first political appointment. When a group of visitors from the West needed help, she tried in vain to get the party leader to respond to them. He wanted to brush the group off into Merkel's care. When she protested that she lacked authority because she did not hold any office in the party, he responded by naming her as his spokeswoman on the spot.

When Merkel's political party collapsed in the 1990 election under the weight of a scandal surrounding its leader's links to the all-knowing East German secret police, the Stasi, Merkel emerged unscathed and undeterred, patiently seeking out new ways to be useful amid these changes. She parlayed her ability to connect with reporters, who found her unusually open, if somewhat direct, into an appointment as deputy spokeswoman to the only freely elected East German government, which served from April until October 1990. In those few months, Merkel quickly became an expert on the issues at play and the need for speed in bringing the two former German nations together, whether concerning monetary policy or convincing Margaret Thatcher to drop her deeply held belief that two Germanys were better than one. Merkel established herself as a presence in the brief government, catching the eye of Kohl and using her position to make herself, as she said, "indispensable,"[8] showing that Merkel had not only understood how to spot an opportunity, but how—and when—to create one. Much has been made of the slowness of Merkel's decision-making. But when she needed to act quickly, she knew how to decide. Once she had made a decision, whether it was popular or not, she also knew how to stick with it.

CHOOSE THE MOMENT
TO MAKE YOUR MOVE

After serving four years as minister for women and youth, and another four years as minister for the environment, in 1999, Merkel found herself for the first time on the other side of politics, as a member of the opposition. It was a period of waiting, but one that she used to invest her energies into addressing the issues plaguing her own party as it sought to regroup. A move that would later prove key in paving Merkel's way to the chancellery, although at the time it appeared to be simply the next most pressing task at hand.

She took on a leadership role that saw her organizing election campaigns and party congresses, serving as a connector and coordinator among the various hierarchies in the leadership. At the same time, she began traveling to local chapters, where people would meet for an evening around a table at a bierstube or in a municipal hall in one of the many towns that dot the German countryside. She called these listening tours and viewed them as a chance to better understand the party's roots and make herself known to the members whose job was to decide who should become their leader—a question that would become more pressing than anyone could at that moment fathom.

That December, investigators in southern Germany uncovered evidence that under Kohl the Christian Democrats had a system of secret accounts to receive what amounted to illegal campaign contributions. Under pressure, the former chancellor admitted weeks later that his party had kept a slush fund, holding several million German marks. But he denied corruption, refusing to name any of the donors. The revelation roiled the usually staid German political world and opened the door for Merkel.

Kohl may have been the grandfather of German reunification, continually discussed as a potential nominee for the Nobel Peace Prize and considered one of the great statesmen of his generation. In addition to being Germany's longest-serving chancellor—a record that he holds to this day—he was the man who had elevated Merkel, supporting her political career, recognizing her sharp political instincts when many focused only on her flowing skirts and leather-strap sandals. But Merkel, driven by the principle of maintaining party integrity, broke with her former mentor. In an op-ed published in Germany's leading conservative daily, the *Frankfurter Allgemeine Zeitung*, she openly called for her party to make a clean break from its longtime leader. "It is about Kohl's credibility, it is about the credibility of the CDU, and it is about the credibility of political parties as a whole,"[9] she wrote, casting the move as necessary if the party ever hoped to return to power.

It was also necessary if Merkel was to seize power. Not only the former chancellor, but all the men who had supported and hoped to succeed him were tarnished. "Such a process does not happen without leaving wounds, without injury," Merkel conceded. But she called for the party's members to see the move as a "necessary, flowing further development."

Prominently displayed on page 2, the piece was a call to arms that rocked Germany's political establishment and propelled Merkel to political prominence. Overnight, media that had previously spent more ink poking fun at her pageboy haircut saw Merkel, the party's second-in-command, not just as "Kohl's girl," the nickname she had been given on her entry into politics, but as a political force in her own right. Merkel had spent her time watching from the sidelines and learning the ropes. For years, she had absorbed the lessons taught by her mentor, who never suspected that when it came time to choose loyalty over party or person, she would choose the party and use the skills he had imparted against him. In true Merkel fashion, she had waited for the exact right time to act.

The night after she had sent the letter to the paper, Merkel couldn't sleep. She alone in Germany knew what was coming the next morning. The day it appeared, she avoided reporters. She waited for the dust to settle and the outrage among Kohl's closest supporters to subside. They were furious at what they saw as a betrayal of the man who towered over the party, defining it for a quarter of a century. But the party's youth wing cheered. So did the members in the small towns who made up the party base that she had spent months listening to at local meetings and town halls. Four months later, they would reward her self-discipline, electing her as their leader and setting her course for the chancellery.

KNOW WHEN TO STAND DOWN

It goes as an unwritten rule that the leader of Germany's conservative Christian Democratic Union runs as the party candidate in an election. But in 2002, just two years after Merkel had been voted party leader, many of her mostly male peers still considered her a placeholder. While they had come around to admiring her courage in calling for change and ousting her former mentor, in their eyes that alone did not make her chancellor material.

When it came time to tap the candidate who would run in the 2002 election against the incumbent, Gerhard Schröder, her peers did not immediately choose Merkel. Instead, they broke with tradition by supporting the leader of the smaller, more deeply conservative Bavarian conservative party that worked together with Merkel's Christian Democratic Union in the parliament in Berlin but maintained its own party structures at home in Bavaria. Merkel thought she had the support of enough leaders in her own party, and it would just be a matter of time. That was until she received a call from one of the men on the party board, informing her that the leaders of her own party were backing her Bavarian rival to run as the conservative candidate for chancellor. Until that moment, Merkel had insisted that she would not back down from her right to run. After all, tradition was on her side.

But by the time she hung up the phone, she understood the situation had changed. She decided that if she was not going to run for chancellor, the decision would be hers. After consulting only her tightest circle, she boarded a charter plane for Munich and demanded a meeting with the Bavarian conservative leader, Edmund Stoiber. He tried to blow her off. He insisted that night wasn't possible because he had a New Year's party to attend that would run until midnight. Meeting afterward would be difficult because it was so late. Merkel insisted, calling his cell phone until he relented, agreeing to meet her the next morning. He invited her for breakfast at eight o'clock, in his home. When Merkel sat down at the table, she showed little interest in the generous spread of fresh-baked bread rolls, honey, jam, and Bavarian sausage, courtesy of Stoiber's wife. Merkel barely even touched her coffee; she was there not to eat, but to make clear that she was ceding the candidacy to her Bavarian rival. She was willing to wait another four years for her chance to run.

It was a painful decision, but Merkel knew that only by taking the upper hand by announcing her decision before the men on her party board could announce theirs would she stand a chance at political survival. When she announced her decision to the media, she smiled and looked relaxed, telling them it felt good to have the matter cleared up. Not only was the move an astute demonstration of her deep understanding of power but yet again proved that she also understood that biding her time, instead of insisting on pressing ahead, could pay off in the long term.

This understanding could be traced back to her years spent studying and analyzing the laws of physics. By applying to her political life the same conservation laws that she knew held true for measured properties such as energy or mass, Merkel remained confident that in time a situation that seemed against her would turn to her advantage, and vice versa. "After downturns, it goes up again," she explained. "And whenever you are highly praised . . . you must already be thinking about the opposite."[10]

HOLD IT TOGETHER

It started as the strains of Germany's national anthem, praising "unity, justice, and freedom for the German fatherland!," wafted over the courtyard of the chancellery, the traditional location for welcoming visiting leaders from other countries. That afternoon in June 2019, the full military honors were for the freshly elected president of Ukraine, Volodymyr Zelensky, on his first state visit to Berlin. Tensions with Russia remained high, five years after the annexation of Crimea, and the new Ukrainian leader had made his frustration with Merkel's refusal to help arm his country and her insistence on maintaining cooperation with Russia clear. But the headlines of the visit barely mentioned the simmering conflict or the young leader, better known as an actor. Instead, the focus was on the chancellor's health.

As she stood to the left of Zelensky in the full afternoon sun, Merkel's legs suddenly started to shake. Her trembling continued as the strains of the music reached higher, spreading upward until her torso, under her pale pink blazer, then her head, became racked, as if an internal earthquake had engulfed her entire body. Merkel clenched her jaw and clasped her hands together, trying in vain to brace herself from the convulsions racking her frame. As she stared straight ahead, trying to act as if everything were normal, the reporters trained their cameras on her trembling frame as the shaking continued unabated for several minutes, rendering the woman largely considered the most powerful leader in Europe utterly helpless. It was a rare position for Merkel, who had mastered the skill of controlling herself in any situation. Whether facing the shouts of "Merkel must go!" from her detractors on the far right or shrugging off the unwillingness of the U.S. president to shake her hand for a photo, the chancellor had always projected an image of cool, calm control. Not that afternoon.

When she appeared before journalists for the regular round of questions a short time later, Merkel seemed to be back to her usual self again, smiling and insisting that "several glasses of water" had restored her. But days later, her body started trembling again, this time at an event indoors, at the presidential palace. Merkel crossed her arms in front of herself, trying to control her body. The image spread like wildfire across social media, shocking people around the globe and raising alarm that the leader widely viewed as the rock of democratic stability could be rendered powerless in the confines of her own body. Publications from Italy's *La Repubblica* to the *Financial Times* all questioned whether after fourteen years in power, the now sixty-four-year-old Merkel had finally reached her limit. Certainly in New York, where memories of how the questions over Hillary Clinton's health had weakened her bid for the White House, people responded with alarm. For the first time, Merkel appeared vulnerable.

Everyone wanted answers. What was causing the shaking? What was she doing to treat it? But Germany has no equivalent of the White House physician. Medical care, and who gives it, is considered a private affair in Germany, even for the chancellor despite the very public nature of the role. And if anyone knew how to protect his or her private life, it was Merkel. Over the following weeks and months, both she and her spokesman brushed off the barrage of questions about the trembling by insisting that it was in her own interest to be healthy. If there was ever a problem that prevented her from carrying out her duties, she would inform the public. Reflecting the trust they had in Merkel, Germans quickly moved on.

Merkel knew she couldn't risk letting it happen again. She had to find a solution or risk damaging her image. She found it in a chair. For weeks, when appearing at a public event where she would normally stand, she instead remained seated. The shaking stopped. So did the questions about her health. After returning from her vacation hiking in northern Italy, she was back to her usual schedule, standing where protocol demanded. By the time she visited China in September, none of us were thinking about her health.

Not until months after she had left office was Merkel willing to speak honestly about the cause of the shaking. By then nearly three years had passed. The world's problems were no longer her responsibility, and faced with fierce criticism about her policies toward Ukraine and Russia since

Moscow had launched its full-scale invasion that February, Merkel made
a rare public confession of weakness. The first bout of shaking had been
the result of dehydration and exhaustion linked to having failed to take
the time to fully mourn the passing of her mother that April. "That took
more out of me than I thought," she told the German journalist and
author Alexander Osang, in a moderated discussion before a sold-out
crowd in the Berliner Ensemble Theater. The evening was intended to
be a discussion about the recently published book of her speeches, but
she ultimately used the platform to defend her reputation. Her explanation of the shaking made headlines. But more interesting to me was that
Merkel also made the rare confession about the strain caused by having
hundreds of telephoto camera lenses trained on her. The thought that
her every move was being observed, later to be parsed by the world, had
added to the stress, she said. "In the end, it was actually a kind of fear that
such a situation could arise again."[11]

Such an acknowledgment could never have been made while she was
still in office. Her critics would have pounced on it as an opportunity to
question her ability to maintain control and fitness for the chancellorship. But six months after stepping down, at a time when her country
appeared eager to pin her with blame for having allowed Putin to invade
Ukraine, the explanation instead enhanced her humanity. Even in the
matter of her personal health, Merkel had chosen her moment carefully,
in this case waiting until she felt safe enough to reveal a weakness.

One of Merkel's favorite phrases, which would crop up in her speeches
and remarks, was *in der Ruhe liegt die Kraft*, roughly translated as "control comes from staying calm." It was a maxim that she not only enjoyed
quoting, but one that defined how she governed and lived.

Chapter 3

KNOW WHERE
YOU COME FROM

Weeks before the Berlin Wall went up, Angela Merkel spent her summer vacation squished into the back seat of a Volkswagen Bug touring Bavaria. It was the summer of 1961, and her grandma in Hamburg, her mother's mom, had wanted to celebrate Grandma's birthday with a road trip to the forests and snowcapped mountains of Bavaria. Merkel's father agreed to drive, so her family made their way to Hamburg. There, Merkel, her parents, and her brother all piled into Grandma's Bug and headed south down the autobahn.

On their way back home, they drove through the hills that today form the heart of Germany. Back then a thirty-two-foot-wide strip slashed through the communities and countryside, a "special demarcation line" drawn by the East German authorities in the 1950s allegedly to keep out spies and other unwanted visitors. But Merkel's father noticed large coils of barbed wire sitting in the woods, interspersed along the line. Merkel remembered hearing her dad tell his mom about it when they stopped off to visit her in East Berlin before making their way home to Templin, the lakeside town north of the German capital where he served as a Lutheran pastor. "Something is going to happen," he said. "I can feel it."[1]

Days later, his premonition came true. On the morning of August 13, 1961, the world awoke to the news that East German authorities had unspooled more than thirty miles of barbed wire along the boundary that roughly defined Berlin's East and West sides. Days later, the same authorities would order workers to begin slathering bricks with cement and stacking them into a crude barricade that would grow in size and stature over the next twenty-eight years, becoming the defining barrier of the bitterly opposed ideologies that divided Berlin, Germany, and the world. That day would sear itself into a seven-year-old girl's mind as her first political memory. Little did she know, as she watched her mother sobbing in the pew at church that morning, that the event triggering those tears was also setting her on a political journey, one that would carry her to the U.S. houses of Congress, Harvard Yard, and the White House Rose Garden. At each place, she would be celebrated as an envoy of democracy, as a representative of the very freedoms being snatched from her that summer morning.

Cut off from her grandmother, her aunts, and her cousins in the West, Merkel would remain keenly aware of the opportunities afforded them by the simple fact of geography, that they lived on the other side of the Iron Curtain. The strength of those ties as she defined her identity, along with her father's role as a pastor in a Lutheran church that harbored dissidents and earned the eternal skepticism of East Germany's Communist leaders, meant that she saw herself from an early age as an outsider. This view helped her when as a young woman she found herself the only woman among the top-level research scientists and, years later when she stood along among the men of the Group of Eight of the world's leading industrial powers. Certainly her ability to absorb and retain detailed information and her analytical approach to problem-solving influenced the leader she would become. Yet those traits traced their roots to her formative years growing up with the understanding that in many ways she might be different from those around her, and being taught that meant she had to be better than them.

A GERMAN-GERMAN
THIRD-CULTURE KID

President Barack Obama is often considered the world's highest-profile third-culture kid, as the son of a Kenyan father and a white American mother who spent time in Indonesia as a child. Those experiences, living outside the United States and reconnecting with his father's family in Africa before he found his place working as a Black man in inner-city Chicago, helped him to develop a bipartisan view that angered both the right and the left. Too liberal for the those on the right, but not nearly progressive enough for those on the left. His attempts to see things from all sides frustrated many, although anyone who has grown up embracing multiple cultures, languages, or identities can relate.

Angela Merkel's multiple identities were not so obvious. She grew up speaking German at home and in school, although she excelled in her mandatory Russian lessons and her mother taught her English. Both of her parents were German, but Merkel's strong ties to her relatives in West Germany meant that she carried in her a duplicity not uncommon in East Germany—the Berlin Wall severed countless families—but one that she felt keenly.

Weeks before she was born, Merkel's father decided the family would leave West Germany to settle in the East. More than 184,000 people[2] would flee in the opposite direction the year that Merkel's mother, Herlind, packed Angela into a basket—this was 1954, less than a decade after the end of World War II, and baby strollers were a luxury that not every family could afford—and carried her over the inner-German border to the East. With that move, Merkel's parents unknowingly bestowed on their infant the first of the multiple identities that would come to shape her life. It would be decades before the term *third-culture kid*, coined by American sociologist Ruth Useem, meaning children who are raised in a culture other than that of their parents, would take hold in popular culture. Merkel's cultural divisions may not seem as obvious, since both of her parents were German and she grew up in a culture with the same language as they spoke. But as Angela Merkel grew, so did the divide between the freethinking, capitalist West Germany and the conformist, Communist East Germany.

It wasn't only Merkel and her siblings who knew they were different. As a pastor's family in a Communist state, the Kasners were all constantly aware they didn't quite belong, or, as Merkel put it, "We were always the outsiders."[3] What may have seemed a struggle while growing up later proved an invaluable life skill. From that early age, Merkel learned to cope with the idea that she didn't conform to the world around her. She learned not to stake her personal value on her ability to conform, but on her ability to assess the strengths of others to enable and work with them. In her life as a physics student, where she was often the only woman, or her later life in the conservative party, where she often stood out as the lone member from the former East on top of being the only woman, Merkel never let it hold her back. She owned her uniqueness, using it as an asset and a way to get ahead.

SEE THE WORLD FROM BOTH SIDES

The wall that severed Berlin wasn't the only dividing line in Angela Merkel's childhood. There was the separation from society that came with being the daughter of a Lutheran pastor growing up in a country where churches were only ever tolerated, but not welcomed. Then there was the compound where her father moved the family when she was three. Called Waldhof, which loosely translates to "forest farm," it was founded in the nineteenth century as an orphanage. By the time young Angela and her family moved in, the place had become a home for people with special needs, both physical and mental, who could not live independently. The Communist authorities saw no place in society for such people, so the churches cared for them in facilities such as Waldhof. There, they were taught to tend the gardens or work in carpentry or crafts, providing them not only with a home and community, but a purpose in life.

The state was more than happy to be relieved of the burden of caring for them, but whenever they ventured beyond the confines of Waldhof, even into town, people were not always welcoming. To young Angela, and to her younger brother, Marcus, and baby sister, Irene, the people who shared the compound with their family were simply their friends. The people always had time for the children and shared with them the daily rhythms of a life informed by the rituals of the church and the practicalities of running a farm. Every morning, a bell on the grounds would sound for the start of the day, then again at noon for the midday meal, with a final ringing in the evening, when Merkel and her siblings knew they had to be back at home. After she had graduated and moved away to university in Leipzig, Merkel keenly missed the tolling of the bell, which had until then helped her to adjust her day with the sonorous reminder of the passage of time.[4]

Years later, once she entered politics and settled in a top-floor apartment in the heart of Berlin, across the water from the German capital's Museum Island, where she still lives today, Merkel bought a modest country home in the region where she grew up, known as the Uckermark. The area is vast and slightly rolling, with a sky that hangs low over the fields and with woods thick with old-growth beeches tangled with paths that open onto pristine lakes that reflect the blue or gray of the sky in glassy brilliance. Years before she became chancellor, Merkel would invite colleagues to her country home. There she would cook for her guests, often using the potatoes or salad ingredients grown in her garden. Afterward, they would make their way down to the lakeshore and jump in for a swim, as Merkel had done on summer evenings as a child.

As the demands on her time grew, the longer she stayed in office and the more frequently she flew to Asia, Africa, or Washington, the more important the rituals of her place in the country, affectionally called her *dacha*, Russian for a "summer cabin," which East Germans adopted. There, she could contemplate how she would bring her fractious coalition together or drum up more solidarity among her European partners for her attempt to share the burden of migrants arriving to Europe. Or she could simply free the potatoes planted in her garden from the tangle of weeds growing up among their stems as she had been taught by one of the gardeners at Waldhof.

Throughout her years as chancellor, Merkel had continued to visit the town, often attending church with her mother, until she passed away in 2019. By that time, many of the town's residents had turned against Merkel's politics, especially her refusal to shut the borders to hundreds of thousands of people who had fled to Germany seeking refuge. Ironically, the roots of her humanitarian, Christian approach to the many migrants could be traced back to the lessons imparted in her during her childhood at Waldhof on the outskirts of Templin. The men and women who lived there not only happily answered her questions but also showed her how to weed a garden, instilling in her a love of digging up a potato that never left her, even during the years she spent hours poring over documents in the chancellery. Through their attention and patience, the inhabitants of Waldhof imparted to Merkel the essential lessons of the gift of time and the understanding that every individual in a society has something to contribute. It is the role of leaders to create an environment where it is possible for them to do so.

It was not until she started school that Merkel was confronted with a radically different image of Waldhof and its inhabitants. When she wanted to invite a friend over to play, their parents would often refuse. Initially, Merkel could not understand their fears. She did not view the people who shared Waldhof with her as threatening, or even disabled. They were individuals with their own physical or mental challenges that

KNOW WHERE YOU COME FROM

required one to slow down and interact differently with them, to meet them where they might be at the time, in the same way they had treated her in her youngest years. As she matured and her capabilities began to exceed those of the adults who had given her their time and attention when she was a child, she did not reject them, but accepted and respected the roles that they carried out as part of the place that she knew as her home. "For me it was all very normal," she said.[5]

For the wary residents of Templin, it obviously was not. Their misgivings toward the people whom Merkel saw as friends would warn her how fears of others could turn into rejection. That experience returned to haunt Merkel in 2015, when hundreds of thousands of migrants who had made their way on foot to Europe found themselves trapped in the tunnels below and around the central train station in Budapest. They demanded the right to march to Germany, singing stadium-worthy chants of the chancellor's name and waving pictures of a smiling Merkel along with the German flag. She relented, and buses and trains were sent to fetch the weary travelers. Their arrival at the Munich train station was met with applause, food, and gifts. But not all Germans celebrated their arrival.

For every older German woman capable of overlooking that the new arrivals wore headscarves and prayed to a different God several times a day and instead saw in the lines of their weary faces the same exhaustion and longing for peace that had defined her own family when they had been forced to flee from their homes in lands ceded to Poland after World War II or from East Germany to the West, there was another who saw only the differences. In their eyes, the new arrivals' dark skin and strange language meant it would be difficult to understand them. Worse, their material desperation meant they would become dependent on the welfare system, which many Germans at that time, especially in the former East, saw as unable to provide for their families and children. The fear toward the new arrivals rooted most deeply in the smaller towns of the former East German states, their residents frustrated by decades of seeing their society dismantled and then redefined by the much-larger and wealthier West Germans. Instead of accepting the number of refugees dictated by Germany's national policy of distributing refugees to communities throughout the country, these residents blocked the roads so buses bringing the refugees could not get through and set fire to shelters prepared to house them.

When Merkel traveled to a community in the former East where angry citizens had for several nights in a row attacked a shelter, and the police assigned to guard it, the citizens turned out to shout and swear at the chancellor. After spending time speaking with those who had fled in hopes of finding a better life in Germany, Merkel stepped outside to a sound wall of whistles, insults, and aggression. As the crowd behind a cordon of police called her a "traitor" and a "whore," Merkel calmly praised those citizens who had donated clothing and were doling out food to the new arrivals. "There is zero tolerance for those who are unwilling to help where help is legally and humanly needed," she said, speaking into a bank of microphones, her voice slightly louder, her diction crisper, to be heard above the din. "The more we make that clear, the stronger we will be."[6] It was a version of a phrase that she would use over and over during the heady weeks that summer. Faced with the mounting anger by many of her people against her stance on immigration, Merkel never wavered. As a child she had felt upset when the townspeople of Templin treated the men she knew as mentors and friends with belligerent ignorance but had been powerless to respond. As chancellor, when thousands of people fleeing conflict and war met with a similar response from some groups, Merkel offered protection for the vulnerable.

ACCEPT CONVENTION,
BUT DON'T CONFORM

Roll call on the first day of school every year was the worst. All pupils were expected to state not only their name, but their parents' professions, another realm into which the long arm of the centralized government extended its reach. Since 1952, East Germany had officially declared itself to be the "State of Workers and Farmers." The government lionized those people who contributed to the public well-being through those fields, as well as their children.[7] Others were viewed with suspicion, especially members of the clergy.

More than once, Merkel considered mumbling her response to make it sound as if her father were no different from the other kids' dads. In German, the only sound separating the word for "driver," *Fahrer*, and the word for "pastor," *Pfarrer*, is an extra *p*. But the difference in how those professions were viewed in the GDR was worlds apart. Drivers were part of the working class, people who did their bit to keep things running, getting goods to market in sputtering trucks or shoveling onto doorsteps the briquettes of coal that people used to heat their homes. Pastors, on the other hand, contributed nothing valued by the East German leaders. They wanted people to turn their backs on religious teachings and spiritual beliefs, considered "opium for the people," and instead learn and embrace the ideologies of Marx and Lenin. In the eyes of the authorities, pastors, and by extension their children, were suspicious.

Merkel understood from the earliest age that she was different from most of her peers, whose families embraced the ideals of the socialist state, and learned to carve her own path within the restrictions around her. It helped that her parents led by example. Many pastors forbade their children from taking part in the state-run social organizations for children, including the scouting organizations linked to the party that formed the backbone of children's social lives in elementary and later into middle school. But Horst Kasner left it up to his kids whether they wanted to take part in the Pioneers in elementary school and, once they turned fourteen, the Free German Youth, known by its German initials as the FDJ. Merkel decided as a schoolgirl to opt in. In school, she would sing "Unsere Heimat," an East German children's song praising the birds in the sky and the fish in the rivers as belonging to the people.

But behind the closed doors of her own home, Merkel and her family rebelled against the strictures of the world around them. Literary classics smuggled in from the West lined their bookshelves. Freedom of the press was guaranteed by the constitution of the GDR, but the authorities had to approve what the country's eighty publishers were actually allowed to print and put into circulation. Approval was withheld for any works deemed "hostile" to the socialist project. Other works could fall under authorities' red pens on grounds they were "negative-decadent," a conveniently vague enough term to include any number of works, including those by internationally recognized authors such as Franz Kafka and Günter Grass, or the Soviet dissident Aleksandr Isayevich Solzhenitsyn, whose novels shed a light on the political oppression in the Soviet Union. But Merkel's father encouraged his daughter to read the works.

Merkel's family also "watched West," an idiom for East Germans who tuned in each night for the news broadcast by West German public television stations, not the evening report that the top Communist, Erich Honecker, personally signed off on every evening. Teachers in the East were trained to "spy" on families' habits by asking their young students to sing the song they heard every night on the evening news. Those who hummed the jingle from the West German stations could expect a visit to their families from the police. Merkel and her siblings had, of course, been drilled in the dangers of such traps. By the time they started school, they knew that it might be risky to fib about your father's profession, but under no circumstances could they let anyone, even their friends, know about the TV shows they watched, political jokes that they told, or thoughts they openly debated.

Beyond giving Merkel the sense of being different, the reality that her family held different beliefs from those of the society in which they moved instilled in her a deep sense of suspicion of others—especially rivals—and an innate need to defend her private life. In her fierce defense of her private life, especially when faced with a public in the social media age that expected world leaders to fire off their thoughts in 140 characters or less, Merkel maintained a highly curated, rather dull social media presence, dominated by pictures of her on the job and clips of her speeches. But she refused to pose for reporters anywhere near her home and demanded that anyone allowed to get close to her uphold her rule of never revealing details to the press. The rare individual who dared to was swiftly cut out of the inner circle.

KNOW THE PRICE OF FREEDOM

Pastors in the East lived off paltry salaries supplemented by care packages from parishes in the West and by growing their own food. Before settling at Waldhof, Merkel's mother had learned to tend a garden, milk goats, and boil for soup the nettles that grew wild around the family's first home in East Germany.

They also relied on packages filled with everyday necessities and hand-me-down clothes sent to them from parishioners in the West. This created the irony that pastors' families, among the poorest members of East German society, often used items that were nearly impossible to get in East Germany, such as laundry detergent and other household essentials that were considered luxuries. And they dressed in coveted Western jackets and jeans—an advantage particularly prized by young people desperate in a country where clothes were cut for durability and practicality. Making a fashion statement was more than just an act of the imagination; it often required the ability to sew your own clothes.

Merkel's family not only had fellow Lutherans on the other side willing to help them out; they also had family. Merkel's grandmother, aunts, and cousins had remained in contact from Hamburg, even after the Berlin Wall was built. They would visit and write regularly, keeping those in the East up-to-date on the politics and fashions driving discussions on the other side. They also sent packages and, more important, they took requests. "Like many other teenagers, I was crazy for a certain brand of jeans that you could not get in the GDR that my aunt in the West would send me regularly," Merkel recalled during her first address to the U.S. Congress decades later.[8] Those were American jeans, and she wore them as a link to a place that held a promise for her: a promise that, if life became too difficult or the politics too intolerable in East Germany, there was always somewhere else she could go.

"There was nothing binding me to the country, and I always thought, if I can't live here anymore, I won't let the system ruin my life, egoist that I am," she said of her life in East Germany as a young woman. "I will go West."[9]

Instead, she went east. As a young teenager, Merkel had excelled at Russian, the required foreign language in East German schools. After school, she would hang around chatting with the Soviet soldiers who were stationed in Templin. At fifteen she became one of her country's youngest winners of the Russian Olympiad, an annual language competition held across the former Soviet Union and its satellite states. It won her a trip to Moscow, as part of the festivities marking the centennial of Lenin's birth. What Merkel remembered most from that trip, however, was linked to her second linguistic love. On that trip to the Soviet capital, she bought her first Beatles album, *Yellow Submarine*.[10]

Whether it was listening to the Beatles nonstop after that, or the help of her mother, a certified English teacher, whom the East German authorities wouldn't hire because she had been trained in the West, Merkel managed to learn English without any classes at school. One of Merkel's favorite pastimes when visiting her grandmother in East Berlin was to hang around outside the Friedrichstrasse train station, where tourists on day trips from the West would cross over. Approaching them, she would offer to give them a tour of the city's museums and serve as a translator, at the same time improving her own language skills and expanding her vocabulary and enhancing her fluency. She was also testing herself, trying to find out if she was as smart as they were, although she had been raised in a system that set limits on what could be learned and who should learn it. "When I had contact with people from the West, I was always testing whether I could keep up with them intellectually,"[11] Merkel recalled. She could, as she would later prove as the newly appointed minister for the environment, communicate confidently and easily in English, as at the early climate summits held by the United Nations, when she stunned her aides, who had been used to her predecessor—a West German—always needing an interpreter on hand.

Knowing that she could hold her own against her peers in the West was satisfaction enough, so that she never tried to smuggle herself over the Berlin Wall or use a visit to her Hamburg family to flee. She also knew that if she defected, the East German authorities might take out their anger on her family members left behind, and she did not want to risk their safety. So she stayed, planning to take the trip to the United States after she retired.

She didn't have to wait that long. After the Berlin Wall fell, Merkel flew to California, where she and her then partner, whom she would later marry, spent four weeks exploring the state and marveling at the power of the Pacific Ocean. In September 1991, as the newly appointed minister for women and youth in Chancellor Helmut Kohl's government, she made her debut visit to the White House, where she met President George Bush Sr., whom she credited for "recognizing the meaning of the historic moment and granting us his trust and support"[12] as the two German nations rushed to reunify the year after the Berlin Wall came down.

Throughout her long years in office, the image of the California sunset seemed to lurk behind Merkel's inner vision of the United States. Despite her frustration at the inability of President George W. Bush, and then President Obama, to close the prison at Guantánamo Bay, despite differences of opinion with Washington over whether it was better for Europe to spend or save its way out of a financial crisis, and even despite President Trump's willingness to tear up the Paris Agreement, aimed at limiting human-generated global warming, Merkel never lost her view of that California sunset. Throughout her sixteen years she remained fascinated—even when frustrated—with the United States as the mother of all democracies and its promise of individual freedom.

In her speech to the Harvard class of 2019, Merkel recalled her frustration at a life hemmed in not only by the physical barrier of the Berlin Wall, but a system that dictated to individuals how they should live their lives—complete with a secret police and a web of informants to enforce the system. When she was a child, the protected world at Waldhof and its leafy surroundings, combined with her parents' strong belief in cultivating independent thinking, had provided a protected environment where Merkel was able to ground herself in the daily rhythms of farm life and reflect on the value of the individual spirit. By the time she reached adulthood, she realized that her hometown was too small to support the vast curiosity of her expanding mind.

At fifteen, she began donning her backpack and boarding trains that carried her to the capitals of other Soviet satellite countries, Prague, Budapest, Bucharest, and Sofia. Later she would hitchhike with friends through the southwestern rim of the then Soviet Union—Georgia, Armenia, and Azerbaijan—using her command of Russian to charm her way into a longer visa. But her travels could only take her toward the east. By the time the authorities trusted her to travel to a wedding in the West in the late 1980s, Merkel's ties to her family in the former East Germany and her life there ran deep. She may have longed to stand on a beach in California and contemplate the vastness of the Pacific Ocean, but not at any price. The pull of her home in the Uckermark ran too deep. "This is where I come from, this is where my roots are," she told a room filled with old classmates, friends, and city leaders in Templin. "And this is where they will always be."[13]

Chapter 4

DON'T LET LIMITATIONS
STOP YOU FROM LIVING

How quickly we are despondent
when something doesn't work.
—ANGELA MERKEL, 2017[1]

When Angela Merkel moved to East Berlin in 1978 as a young wife, it didn't matter that she and her husband both had solid jobs as research scientists—apartments were still hard to find. Much like today, friends and contacts were the best way to find a place, and you took whatever you could. At that time, one of the least desirable places in the East German capital were the apartment buildings in the shadow of the heavily fortified concrete barrier that divided the city—and ultimately Europe and the world. But that is where the young couple found their home, throwing Merkel into a constant, if muted, confrontation with the West. The seemingly intractable presence of the Berlin Wall defined the first years of Merkel's adult life. From the start of her day, when she began her commute at the Friedrichstrasse train station, the main crossing point for Germans traveling between East and West Berlin, the tracks served as a forced, unnatural boundary between the two sides of the city. From the platform where she boarded her train, she could hear dogs barking. But she couldn't see them because they were on the opposite platform, mere feet away from her, but in another country, in West Berlin.

Her commute took her along the Spree River, which served as the boundary between the two sides of the divided city as you traveled toward the eastern suburbs. As you looked out the window, the gray concrete barrier—only on the western side were graffiti artists allowed to decorate it with artwork and protest slogans—snaked along, a visible reminder of the Communist system and the limitations that it imposed on the lives of the roughly 16 million people who lived in East Germany. Their abilities to cope were varied. Some rebelled against it. Some risked their lives to escape it. Others, such as Merkel, found ways to adapt, accepting the constraints on expression and travel while embracing the beauty found in time spent with family and friends, on hikes through the forests and trips to the theater.

Decades later, Merkel would spend most of her working hours just blocks away from her first home in the German capital. Only instead of making a home in a cramped apartment, she would host global leaders in the towering, angular concrete chancellery building—nicknamed the "federal washing machine" by Berliners for the rounded glass windows in its square frame that resembled a giant front-loading washer. The balcony off the main reception room offered Merkel a view over her old neighborhood, now emerged from the shadows as the heart of a bustling, cosmopolitan European capital.

When Queen Elizabeth paid her a visit at the chancellery in 2015, Merkel escorted her out onto the balcony, with its expansive view of the former strip of no-man's-land, now home to the seat of the German government. Merkel pointed out the sights. There was the embassy of Switzerland, which had refused to relocate, even when it found itself in the dead zone between the two nations; the Reichstag, now restored to its former glory and topped with a gleaming glass dome designed by the British architect Norman Foster; and the elevated railway tracks that snake their way through the heart of the city. "Where the train goes there, there was the Wall. And I lived in East Germany just two hundred meters behind it."[2] The queen nodded, and as Merkel explained, a smile spread across her face as if in that moment she recognized the irony of the ridiculously small physical distance that separated her, as chancellor of reunited Germany, from her former life in a tiny apartment in the shadow of the Berlin Wall.

In her early years in politics, Merkel spoke frequently and willingly of her life growing up in the former East Germany. But as the demands on her time mounted, it seemed to recede into history, a past that neither she, nor most Germans, were eager to revisit. Not until her final speeches as chancellor did she return to the topic, pushing back against the negative perception of those Germans who spent their formative years under the repressions of a dictatorship as unable to fully embrace democracy and its gift of possibility. It was a complaint I heard from many of my friends who had grown up in the former East, that an overwhelmingly negative popular narrative of their past had seeped into the general German consciousness. They felt a disconnect between this version of history and their memories of the lives they had actually lived, with their small joys of gatherings with friends, family rituals, and daily rhythms that all took place beyond the strictures of the political system and even the all-present spying of the state secret police.

Another common complaint focused on the idea that German society failed to honor the efforts that East Germans had invested in ultimately securing their own freedom. While President Ronald Reagan may have stood at the Brandenburg Gate, still behind the Berlin Wall, in 1987 demanding that Mr. Gorbachev "tear down this wall," it was the hundreds of thousands of East Germans who took to the streets two years later, night after night risking their lives, who ultimately accomplished that feat. It was a revolution decades in the making. But one that sprang up from the grass roots of communities and congregations across the country that culminated in achieving the unthinkable.

Merkel understood. She had attended discussions among dissidents in the summer before the mass demonstrations had brought the Wall down. Even then, her powers of observation dominated over her willingness to act. Although she attended meetings of dissidents that her father hosted in the safety of their living room at Waldhof, she chose not to join the loudest voices criticizing the government. Instead, she observed. She listened and she thought. She had smuggled in forbidden protest writings from the Polish Solidarity movement's push against their government and closely followed reports from the West on her own country. Merkel would later call the collapse of Communism a surprise, as well as a gift. But at her deepest levels, even as she questioned its viability, she had been toying with the possibility for years. The lessons that she took from that pivotal moment in history would grow into one of her seminal beliefs. "Anything that seems to be set in stone or inalterable can indeed change" is how she explained it to the graduates at Harvard in 2019. "In matters both large and small, it holds true that every change begins in the mind."[3]

MAKE THE RULES WORK FOR YOU

"I long for the feasible," Merkel said in an early interview broadcast on German national public television in 1991.[4] The feasible, for Merkel, could be identified as that which can be accomplished, the best possible solution that kept all parties involved on board. As leader of the center-right party needing support from another political party to form a government, that meant making concessions to an erstwhile rival party on the center left. As the head of state considered the de facto leader of Europe, that meant seizing on the feeling of great uncertainty, as the world emerged from the lockdowns aimed at slowing the spread of the coronavirus, to cross a previous red line for her country. She allowed Germany to take on the shared debt of its economically weaker partners in the European Union. Just several years earlier, as Europe floundered through the depths of a debt crisis that crippled Greece, the move had been a no-go. Germans had insisted that taking on the debt of weaker European partners would weaken their own economic prosperity. But

Merkel understood the importance of timing. The political moment post-coronavirus presented her with an opportunity to make a move within the system, stretching it ever so slightly beyond the boundaries of the previously acceptable, but without taking it too far. It was a skill she had picked up in her days as a squatter in East Berlin.

It wasn't that she was trying to join the punks. It was the early 1980s and she had just packed her bags and left her first husband, a fellow physics student she had met in Leipzig. But their lives in the East German capital had gone separate ways; she liked going out with friends and to the theater, he preferred to stay home. One day in 1981, he returned to their apartment near the Berlin Wall to find she had packed her bags. For the first few nights, a friend let her crash on his couch, but she needed to find a place of her own. Because apartments were allocated by the state, none wanted to give up their leases, even if they'd vacated a place and moved out. Often, they would pack up their personal belongings and simply lock the door behind them, never letting the government know they no longer lived there. Apartments could sit empty for years. But in a country that rewarded people for spying on their neighbors, after several months of vacancy most neighbors who shared a wall (the crumbling plaster meant you could easily hear what the person next door was up to) or at least a stairwell knew which places were occupied and which were empty.

A friend of Merkel's knew of such an unofficially abandoned apartment in a tumbledown prewar building on Templiner Street in the Prenzlauer Berg district, where the Berlin Wall formed its boundary to the west. Together with several friends, Merkel broke into the place, swapped out the lock, and brightened the walls with a fresh coat of white paint.

Relieved to have a place of her own, Merkel set about making sure that she could keep it. Since the East German government regulated rents, and her previous apartment had come with a contract, she made a few calculations and came up with an estimate of how much she thought she owed for her new place. Armed with a story about the serendipity of finding an apartment on a street named for her hometown of Templin, she headed to the registrar's office and offered to pay the amount she had calculated in rent. Critics would often fault Merkel for lacking a grand vision for Germany and Europe, attributing that shortsightedness to her having grown up in a dictatorship. What many failed to see was the subtle ingenuity that she had developed as a way to find the cracks within its strictures to meet her own needs and withstand its ability to crush an individual's spirit.

YOUR MOST VALUABLE RESOURCE IS TIME

In January 1992, Angela Merkel had not only achieved her goal of serving in reunited Germany's first parliament, but she had also been named minister for women and youth in the first unified government. Amid the excitement came the stress of a steep learning curve of being a freshman lawmaker and junior minister in a system new to her. One friend, a fellow East German who had fled to the West more than a decade before the Berlin Wall collapsed, recalled spending an evening with Angela, lying on the floor of his parents' house, surrounded by books and diagrams that detailed the ins and outs of the political system. She had so much to learn, on the fly, while running a ministry and drawing up legislation. That winter, she slipped and broke her leg in several places, landing her in the hospital for weeks. After months of running to keep pace with unexpected events that had begun with the fall of the Berlin Wall and ended with her serving in government, she found herself in the unique situation of being required to slow down. "Lucky in misfortune" was how she described it.[5]

In the same way that the coronavirus lockdowns led many people to reconnect with old friends, take up baking, or watch the series they had until that point never made the time for, Merkel took advantage of her imposed immobility to catch up on reading and to process the political life that she had, until that point, been living at breakneck speed. Her previous life had had a predictable familiarity. During Berlin's long winter months, when the sun does not rise until around eight o'clock in the morning and sets by four thirty in the afternoon, Angela Merkel would often leave home in the dark and after hours spent in the laboratory return in the dark. Along the way she would grab the papers, including the main Russian-language daily, *Pravda*, if she was early enough to snag one of the few available copies. Once in her office, she would brew a thick Turkish-style coffee, boiling the grounds and some sugar in a tiny pot on the stove, before pulling the plastic protective sleeves over the arms of her sweater to prevent any chemicals from eating away at the threads.

Over the course of a decade, her days flowed together in a familiar rhythm with ample space for reading novels and political speeches smuggled in from the West, debating the state of the East German economy with friends, and visiting the sauna every Thursday evening. Not until after the euphoria of German reunification had subsided would Merkel have time to look back and reflect on the benefits of her old life. Despite all of the burdens of the limitations of a life under a controlling state, the absence of so many choices had left a spaciousness that it would take until she left office to find again. Looking back, Merkel would realize that the boring predictability of that life had brought with it an element that she would come to miss: free time.

By the time that she found herself stuck in the hospital with her leg in traction, her life had been taken over by the demands of politics. At that time, Merkel's version of unwinding and decompression was not to spend a night binging on a Netflix series, but grabbing tickets to the opera. She would specially make time for performances of her favorite opera, Richard Wagner's *Tristan and Isolde*, a romantic drama based on the tale of a medieval romance between a king's daughter and her lover. Music from the score was also used in the second season of Netflix's drama of the British royal house, *The Crown*, which Merkel—having met Queen Elizabeth II, the protagonist of the series, several times—watched during the six months after she had left the chancellery.

Although thick government-issued folders holding the briefing notes collected by her advisers had replaced novels as her regular reading during her time in office, she still made time for nonfiction works that were driving the public discourse. Often she would cite those volumes she found inspiring. She often cited the British bestseller *The Sleepwalkers: How Europe Went to War in 1914*, by Christopher Clark, when defending her decision to keep speaking to President Vladimir Putin after Russia illegally annexed the Crimean Peninsula from Ukraine in 2014. She found President Obama's *Dreams from My Father* an inspiring insight into the mind of the man who began as a fellow leader and became a close friend. She also read Michelle Obama's story of how she planted a garden at the White House, *American Grown*.

Merkel was such a fan of the books by award-winning German historian Jürgen Osterhammel, an expert in the theories of globalism, that she not only made time to read them but tapped him to serve as the entertainment for the guests invited to her sixtieth birthday party. To a woman who had smuggled books across borders at a time when they were forbidden, what better way to celebrate than with a lecture on globalization throughout the centuries? Merkel often remarked that one failing of modern politics was that individuals who had experienced life and professions outside of lawmaking were often underrepresented. That they also lacked her own burning curiosity and intellectual hunger was made obvious when several of those invited simply disregarded their invitations, which had slyly failed to mention the chancellor's birthday, instead advertising the evening simply as a history lecture. They missed out on one of Berlin's most talked about parties of that year.

WHERE YOU CAN'T CHANGE, COMPROMISE

Compromising, for Merkel, constituted the art of understanding how far you could go in a given situation to accommodate others' positions, without betraying yourself. It was a skill she learned early in life. The rigid limitations of the Communist system forced her to balance her hunger for success with the knowledge that all achievements would benefit the state. The political activism of her home and her strong ties to her grandmother, aunts, and cousins in the West meant that she constantly had to find a middle ground between the push and pull of her dueling identities. Then there was the strength of her faith and her life within the Lutheran Church, constantly butting up against her desire to fit in with her peers in a system that prized atheism and conformity to Communist ideals. In young Angela's case the solution was found in joining the Free German Youth organization, which promoted the Marxist-Leninist ideals of the state and was intended to groom future members of the Communist Party. But instead of joining most of her peers in taking part in the traditional coming-of-age ceremony sponsored by the East German state, she chose to be confirmed in the Lutheran Church.

As chancellor, this early-life practice at finding a place within the opposing forces around her led Merkel to become a master at building coalitions. Starting in 2005, when she successfully led her conservative party to find sufficient common ground with their erstwhile rivals to form the first of three coalition governments together, it was considered an unexpected achievement. That constellation, the center-right Christian Democrats governing with the center-left Social Democrats, would become Merkel's default, for three of her four governments. Beyond Germany, Merkel's insistence on personally carrying out shuttle diplomacy in the halls of the European Union became legendary. She would take members aside and sound them out, listening to find points of crossover.

This process did not mean that Merkel always achieved what she personally wanted or maybe even thought was best for the situation. Instead she emphasized finding a solution that acknowledged the interests of everyone involved. One of Merkel's closest friends, who served in several of her governments, Annette Schavan, had a place at the chancellor's negotiating table for years. She witnessed how carefully Merkel would seek to include the opinions of everyone, allowing each person around the table to have his or her say in a decision, so that even those who did not see their ambitions realized would be able to take ownership.

"Time and again we went through situations where the only way that we could do justice to society was to work out a compromise, to strive to do justice to everyone sitting at the table so that in the end, everyone could say, 'I have been able to contribute, my arguments have played a role, even if they have not prevailed'" was how Schavan described Merkel's ability to find a compromise.[6]

CHOOSE YOUR WORDS CAREFULLY

In 2018, when President Trump posted a tweet indirectly targeting Merkel by alleging, "The people of Germany are turning against their leadership as migration is rocking the already tenuous Berlin coalition,"[7] an editor called me from New York. He wanted to know how Merkel had replied. She hasn't, I said, and she won't. "Angela Merkel is not on social media," I told the editor. Not on Twitter, or Facebook or Instagram (TikTok had not yet expanded beyond a handful of tech-savvy teens). He replied in stunned silence. In an age where most all politicians had realized the power of being able to communicate their thoughts directly to the public, the idea of not participating in the great global discussion seemed foolish. But Merkel had decided early on in her career to delegate her presence on social media to her press and public relations team. If she had something she wanted the world to know, she had her spokesman send it out. In the case of the cascade of messages on Twitter that President Trump would fire her way, she simply did not bother.

Not that she wasn't aware of the power of social media. In 2013, when President Obama paid her a visit in Berlin, the two appeared before journalists to respond to questions. At that time, the German capital was still abuzz with the recent revelations that the U.S. National Security Agency had secretly been collecting citizens' data from their mobile phones and the internet. Germans were incensed. After all, here was a country whose people had witnessed their civilization collapse under the weight of Nazi terror, fed by the denunciation of neighbors and coworkers. Those who, like Merkel, had grown up under the watchful eye of the East German state's dreaded secret police, the Stasi, harbored a particular fear of losing control of their personal information. They expected Merkel to take a stand against such American hubris. Instead, when a journalist asked her about the spying, she calmly responded by calling the internet "*Neuland*," or "unchartered territory." To social media users, many of whom had grown up with the internet, which had by that time been around for two decades, this remark provided endless fodder for derision. Users posted images quoting and mocking Merkel's statement—including one featuring the notorious feline Grumpy Cat—across the internet. Her spokesman was forced to clarify that Merkel had used the term in a legal sense, referring to the lack of regulation and rules governing the service at the time.

But the joke did not end there. Five years later, Merkel brought up the incident in a speech to a technology conference. Recalling the statement's impact, she told a self-deprecating anecdote reflecting on how widely she had been mocked (the first time she had acknowledged as much).

"It generated quite a shitstorm," she said, laughing. Unwittingly, the woman who shunned social media had set it alight again. Germans have a maddening habit of adopting English words and infusing them with meanings utterly unknown to the average native English-speaker. The video clip of Merkel dropping a word that still had the power to shock when coming from the mouth of an American or British politician spread across the internet like wildfire. Those of us journalists who speak English wrote articles trying to explain that the chancellor wasn't intentionally trying to sound vulgar, while others simply rejoiced in the seeming incongruity of the woman known as a staid, no-drama leader appearing to let loose her inner rebel. In an age when a woman who is perceived as "particularly strong, who is particularly cool, who is particularly swaggery,"[8] is celebrated as "badass," Merkel may just have been proving her right to wear that badge with pride.

Not that anyone was questioning her claim to the term. That summer she had displayed her command of the power of the internet. As the heads of the world's seven leading industrial countries gathered in Canada to try to find consensus on the world's most pressing issues of the economy, climate change, and clean energy, everyone knew the elephant in the room was the U.S. president and his divergent view of the problems plaguing the world. On the second day of the summit, Merkel's office posted a picture to Instagram that would become the defining image of the meeting and of her relationship to Trump. It showed Merkel, dressed in a sky-blue blazer, both palms pressed against the top of a table, leaning over a piece of paper. From across the table, a defiant President Trump, his arms crossed against his chest, glares back at her while the other men in their dark navy suits—Theresa May, the prime minister of Great Britain and the only other woman in the photo, is largely hidden from view—all appear to be turned toward Merkel, listening intently. The image captured the spirit of the summit and cemented the badass status of the woman at its center. It also allowed Merkel to send a clear message on her personal views of the U.S. president.

As if to assure those who might not have got the message, the next summer Merkel pushed another boundary to make her point. During her vacation in the Italian Alps, she appeared on the balcony of her hotel room one day, unusually well styled for a woman known to fully embrace her out-of-office time by dressing in the same casual outdoor gear year after year. In her hand, she held a book unnaturally high up. Positioned so that the title could be read through the slats of the balcony railing, for any photographers who might have had their long lenses trained to the location, the title was clear: *Tyrant*, by Harvard professor Stephen Greenblatt. The book dissects the leading tyrants of Shakespearean theater in what was widely discussed and understood to be a veiled critique of Trump's presidency.

The leading German weekly newsmagazine, *Der Spiegel,* declared the image a "meta-sign" signaling her concern over the threat posed to liberal values, including freedom of expression."[9] It served as a testament to the fact that even when she chose to speak in pictures, instead of words, Angela Merkel weighed each one carefully.

PROTECT YOUR VALUES

Although many political rivals would insinuate Merkel had had ties to the East German Communist leadership, concrete evidence that she ever cooperated with the regime or helped the Stasi has never been found. Her response to questions about her relationship with the secret police is to recount how her parents drilled into her and her siblings' minds that should they ever be approached by someone trying to recruit them, they should respond by insisting they were too unreliable for such activity. Only once, her story goes, did someone try to recruit her, in 1978. She was applying for a job at the Technical University of Ilmenau, and after she had sat down for an interview with the heads of the department, two men approached her on the stairwell. They pulled her aside for another interview, of an entirely different nature. Their questions began with attempts to figure out whether she consumed media or took part in other activities they considered subversive. Merkel knew immediately who they were and what they wanted. When they asked whether, should she be hired, she would be willing to slip them information on her students and colleagues, she had her response ready.

"You know, I probably can't keep quiet," Merkel told the agents, without missing a beat. Her parents had made sure that their children understood that a good informant had to be circumspect. They should never let on what they had been asked to do—spy on their friends, neighbors, and relatives and report back to the state. The Stasi could not risk a chatterbox. Merkel had got the message. "I most likely can't stop myself from telling my husband about it when I work for you," she told the agents.[10]

Merkel had no illusions that her response had dashed her chances of ever being accepted for the position. But confirming her parents' suspicions, it remained the only time that the Stasi ever approached her. Years after reunification, she would learn that some of her closest colleagues at the Academy of Sciences, including one who shared her office for a time, had fed the Stasi a lot of information about her. Certainly, her office mate would have let the authorities know about what she was up to, especially because the informant would have taken part in, or at least overheard, many of the political discussions that she and her former colleagues had in what she had thought was the relative safety of their office.

Since she began rising in politics in the late 1990s, speculation has swirled around Angela Merkel's relationship to the secret police and her activities in the Free German Youth. But unlike with some of her peers, no damning information has ever surfaced. If such records exist, she has prevented them from being made public, as is her right under Germany's privacy protection laws.

But the absence of a file listing Merkel as an informant did not prevent bogus theories from springing up across the internet. Like Hillary Clinton, who years after stepping down from office is still dogged by allegations of her purported role in pedophile rings and misconceptions surrounding her emails, Merkel has yet to shake the interest of internet trolls.

Perhaps the most persistent theory about Merkel is linked to the lack of a secret file about her life in East Germany. According to the theory, which has found its way into bestselling books and been dissected in leading German news media, instead of rejecting the overtures of the Stasi agents as she recalled, Merkel had served as an informant for them. Her purported code name was I. M. Erika.

During the height of her final years in office, when the public was growing weary of the lockdowns imposed by Merkel's government and her explanations of how the coronavirus spread inspired more frustration than trust, the name I. M. Erika turned up ninety-two thousand times on Twitter alone, according to Hubertus Knabe, a German historian who served as the last director of the archive of documents collected by the Stasi.[11] He noted that the attempts to paint Merkel as a Stasi informant tend to be based more on well-known anecdotes from her past.

Another popular myth appeared shortly after Merkel won her fourth term in office. This one featured a black-and-white photograph of her as a teenager seated beside two other girlfriends. A version that circulated widely through social media at the time, with captions in Arabic, Turkish, Italian, and Russian, identified the two other friends as British prime minister Theresa May and Dalia Grybauskaitė, who served as president of Lithuania from 2009 to 2019. The captions further claimed that the trio had attended a special school where they were "trained for leadership" and then "assigned to specific countries" as part of a sinister global conspiracy.

For Grybauskaitė, who worked alongside Merkel at the European Union, the culprit was clear. By the time that the photo—originally published in *Time* in 2015, when it named Merkel its Person of the Year—began making the rounds, both she and Merkel had spent the previous four years pushing their partners in the EU to tighten the sanctions against Moscow in response to Russia's illegal annexation of the Crimean Peninsula in Ukraine. As the head of a tiny Baltic country that shares a border with Russia, Grybauskaitė used every opportunity possible to warn against the threat Vladimir Putin posed to his neighbors. She told me that she had "at least five biographies," thanks to Russian attempts to discredit her through propaganda. Once Merkel began pushing to punish Russia—even as she kept its natural gas flowing to Germany—she became fair game for a wider circle of conspiracy theorists.

Both women—like their female peers in power from Washington, DC, to Wellington, New Zealand—had quickly learned the level of emotional energy that could be wasted by even acknowledging every version of their lives that popped up online. Most did not reach a level of awareness among the general public to even merit the time it would take to refute them. But the theories about Merkel's recollections of her East German past would occasionally reach the national news, provoking questions that demanded an answer. A book published in 2013 that claimed to have unearthed evidence that she collaborated with the state hit the German bestseller list, reopening questions about whether Merkel had been telling everything or telling the truth about her past. She had to respond. When she did, she chose to answer with a reflection of the same values that had prevented her from cooperating with the secret police as a young researcher, unwilling to compromise her integrity and honesty, even if it meant it would cost her a chance at launching her career. "What is important to me," she said, "I have never kept anything secret."[12]

SET THE RECORD STRAIGHT

Not until October 3, 2021, during what would be her final speech as chancellor at the annual ceremony marking the Reunification Day holiday, did Merkel really open up about how she had felt leading a reunited German nation as someone who had spent her formative years in the former East Germany. She began on familiar ground, speaking about the effort required to maintain a healthy democracy. But then, in an unexpected and uncharacteristic move, she veered off into more personal and emotional territory. For sixteen years, Merkel had refused to go there, looking back into her past and how it had played out in the eyes of a media and a public dominated by the West German lens, throughout the more than three decades she had spent in power.

Now, so near the end of her life in the public eye, she described how she had left the limitations of a dictatorship for the freedom of a democracy, only to find herself bound by stereotypes perpetuated by the world around her. She cited times when she felt that her past had been used against her, pointing out when others had used it to belittle or reduce her achievements as less valuable simply because her life had begun in a dictatorship. She spoke inclusively, driving home the point that her experience was shared by many of the roughly 16 million other former East Germans by stressing that despite having risen to the most powerful position in government, her peers raised in the former West Germany still viewed and valued her life experience as somehow lesser than their own. She cited an article written by a journalist she said she knew and respected. The piece had run the previous year in one of the country's leading Sunday papers and summarized her years in office. It included a reflection on a comment she had made at the height of the 2015 refugee crisis, as public sentiment was tipping from welcoming to rejection: "Then she did something that none of her predecessors in office had ever done before: she distanced herself in one breath from the republic that she served as second-most important servant. She said: If I have to apologize for having shown a friendly face in the refugee crisis, 'then that is not my country.' In that moment, it was clear as a flash that she is not a true-born, but a trainee German and European."[13]

Even as she maintained her controlled pacing, her voice was stung with hurt and disbelief. Here she was, the woman who had attended 107 summits at the European Council, who Anne Applebaum had hailed as the "empress of Europe,"[14] and Barack Obama had praised for playing "a very, very important role in preserving European solidarity and the European idea,"[15] having her credentials as a European questioned because she had not been raised on the border to France or Belgium.

People in the audience squirmed and looked down at their feet. In that moment, Merkel spoke not as the most powerful woman in the world, but as an individual wounded by the stark reality that even within the democracy that she had so desired, she would never be truly free. She had spent sixteen years letting every slight about her past, every question about her integrity, roll off her, often without so much as a remark. But each and every one had registered. And each one had stung.

But Merkel wasn't done. She had chosen her moment carefully, the symbolism of her last Reunification Day celebration, understanding better than many seated in the audience before her the full impact of the mixed elation and pain that had come with the achievement of what had for decades seemed little more than a dream, but at the cost of losing one's home country.

"Are there two types of Germans and Europeans—the original and the trainees, who have to prove their right to belong every day and with a sentence in a press conference can fail the test?" she asked. "Or put another way, because this is the heart of the matter, who decides which Germans understand the values and interest of our country and which don't?"[16]

The audience, a mixture of political leaders and former East Germans, rose to their feet and began applauding as she left the lectern and returned to her seat in the front row. For several minutes, a thunderous, steady rhythm of recognition and respect reverberated through the hall. Merkel, visibly uncomfortable as the clapping continued unabated, sought several times to bring it to an end, first waving, then gesturing at the string orchestra, as if hoping they would begin playing and bring the acknowledgment to an end. Early in her career as a politician, Merkel had felt uncomfortable when a room applauded her. She later learned to accept the German tradition of extended clapping as a sign that she was on the right track, her message had resounded with people she needed to remain in office, whether as political party leader or as chancellor. But this was different. This time, it was a hurt that she had carried with grit and grace in serving her country and doing her job, not a political idea, that was receiving recognition, and she had never felt comfortable with letting the outside world into her innermost personal realm.

By calling out modern Germany for failing to recognize and honor the contributions of its citizens who hailed from the former East, even those such as herself who'd reached the highest levels of power, Merkel had broken through another barrier. For sixteen years, she had stressed the importance of representing all Germans, refusing to single out or acknowledge the specific challenges of the stereotypes and lack of recognition that regularly confronted former East Germans. Over time, people in the former East grew to resent her silence, understanding it as a lack of compassion, and a failure to acknowledge that while she had benefited from the tectonic political shift that came with the fall of the Berlin Wall, others had suffered. With that speech, Merkel made clear that she had chafed against the same prejudices as any other East German. But she had refused to let them define either her person, or her ability to lead.

Chapter 5

EMBRACE THE POWER OF CHANGE

Anything that seems to be set in
stone or inalterable can indeed change.
—ANGELA MERKEL, 2019

Angela Merkel never had any doubts: the events of November 9, 1989, changed her life for the better. She seemed to sense the possibilities promised by the unexpected gift of democracy, and she was willing to work for them. In the earliest days after the Wall came down, she set herself on a course to seize the opportunity that life had unexpectedly thrown at her, leaving behind the regularity of the chemistry lab and the profession she had practiced for years since graduation, and throwing herself into the world of politics. It was a personal transformation, and one she hoped would help shape the new, reunited Germany that was emerging before her eyes.

Not that this was what she was thinking the night that the wall cracked open. It was the time of year of the pale winter light, yellowed from the acrid smog that billowed from the chimneys, rising from the coal-fired stoves still used then to heat homes in East Berlin. When she came home from work, although she knew that tensions had been rising for months, foremost on Merkel's mind was that it was a Thursday, the day when she and a friend visited the local sauna to sit in the hot, dry air long enough to chase the chill from their bones that began to set in every November and seemed to remain until the following spring.

Social media didn't exist, nor did twenty-four-hour television news, so Merkel relied on newspapers and bulletins read over the radio and on the regular nightly TV news programs. "Since October seventh at the latest, you could hear the crackle every day that something was happening, and yet you still couldn't really imagine where it was all going," Merkel recalled in speaking to a group of high school students about how she experienced the night the Berlin Wall crashed open.[1]

Since late summer of that year, thousands of East Germans who were fed up with their leadership and demanding their rights be respected and their voices be heard had taken to the streets in peaceful protests, defying the regime and the police. Such demonstrations posed a direct threat to the control of the East German government over the people, and at any moment the authorities could have ordered the police to use any means to put an end to the public displays of outrage. But they didn't.

Instead, the government sought to appease the demonstrators. The actual opening of the Wall was somewhat of an accident after the government authorities handed a lower-ranking official a prepared text that he was to read out at a press conference. One line of it said that the authorities would begin allowing East Germans to leave the country without needing to meet the previous requirements. Reporters leaped on it and peppered the man with questions. When would that change take effect? Unsure how to manage the situation, and unprepared for the fierce fire of queries, the man shuffled his papers and looked confused. Then, without realizing the full impact his words would carry, he replied, "Immediately."[2]

By 7:00 p.m., news of the possibility to travel was already beginning to spread across the divided city, and the world. Merkel had watched the press conference and understood that East Germans might now be allowed to travel to the West without the previous restrictions. But that thought at the time was so unthinkable. Merkel had returned weeks earlier from a rare trip to West Germany, where she had visited her relatives in the northern city of Hamburg and her partner, a fellow researcher from the Academy of Sciences who was on a grant in the southwestern city of Karlsruhe.[3] She knew the amount of paperwork involved in travel. Just hearing someone on TV say that it was now possible without any of the applications, the scrutiny, the waiting, as she had just gone through was not enough to convince her to change her plans for that evening. It was a Thursday, the night that she had a standing sauna date to keep. But, before leaving her apartment, she picked up the phone and called her mother.

"We used to joke in our family that if the Wall were to disappear one day—although no one believed that it would—we'd go to Kempinski for oysters," she said, referring to the hotel near the main drag that ran through the heart of West Berlin, which had played host to the likes of Sophia Loren, Liza Minelli, and President John F. Kennedy. "I said, 'Watch this, Mother, something is happening.'"[4]

Years later, Merkel would come under criticism for her dithering and waiting, wasting too much time weighing her options, before making her move at the last minute. Many biographers and reporters who had followed her for years traced her deliberations to the scientific methods she had learned and practiced during her first career as a physicist. But even in her earliest childhood, she had displayed what one of her biographers called "the courage of the last second,"[5] the ability to make her move at the last possible moment, before it was too late. That ability, which she would describe as waiting to jump from the diving board until the whistle blew in her sports class at school, could also be seen the night that East Berlin residents demanded their right to cross to the West.

By the time she and her friend left the sauna, people packed the streets of their neighborhood. Everyone surged toward the nearest border crossing, Bornholmer Strasse. The guards there had given in to the crush of people demanding to be let across and opened the gates shortly before midnight. Merkel joined the flow and found herself carried across the heavily fortified border in the rush of euphoric crowds astonished at being caught up in a moment most had never thought they would live to see.

Once across, equally surprised West Berliners greeted the arrivals with bottles of champagne and cans of beer. Spontaneous parties broke out in the streets, and West Berlin residents threw open their homes, eager to welcome their neighbors who, for twenty-eight years, they had been forbidden to meet. Many stayed and partied until the sun came up and into the following days, swept up in the euphoria of finding themselves in the eye of the storm of history and not wanting to miss the celebrations. But Merkel, after having her first West German beer, "in a can, something that I wasn't familiar with at the time," crossed back to East Berlin after several hours.[6] Mindful of the time and knowing that she would be expected to turn up at the Academy of Sciences the next morning, Merkel finished her beer and, ignoring the euphoria around her, crossed back over to her home in East Berlin and crawled into bed. While some might have regretted not staying in the West, or joining in the throngs that climbed atop the Wall in front of the Brandenburg Gate, historically chipping away at its concrete, not Merkel. "I had to be at work early the next morning," she said. "And I was an upstanding person."[7]

It didn't take Merkel many days to realize that the world around her had shifted and she needed to change as well. Before long, she would strike out to find a political home among the parties, new and old, that hosted events in hopes of wooing new supporters among the East Germans. An idea also formed in her head that she wanted to not only experience that new reality taking place around her, but to find a front seat in its events and contribute to the decisions that would shape her own life, and those of millions of other Germans. Merkel would later call the events of late 1989 as the biggest surprise of her life. Until that time, she had only known boundaries that could be bumped against, stretched, but never broken through. Once those limitations were gone, she quickly realized that their absence meant the chance to try new things and reinvent herself. She wasted no time in getting to work.

KNOW WHAT YOUR AUDIENCE
WANTS BEFORE ASKING THEM TO CHANGE

The year that Angela Merkel first ran for the chancellery, more Germans were out of work than at any time since the end of World War II. Nearly 5 million people depended on the country's social system, and the state was struggling to support them. Merkel zeroed in on taxes as one of the reasons for Germany's financial troubles. She tapped a professor and former judge in Germany's highest court to propose a rework to the country's tax code, thinking he could be her secret weapon. Instead, he nearly cost her the election.

His proposed changes were to radically simplify how Germans pay their taxes. But he couldn't explain his concept to voters, instead leaving them confused and Merkel exposed to criticism. The result was widespread uncertainty, and an invaluable opportunity for her opponent, the incumbent chancellor, Schröder, to take her down as incompetent and naïve. Her suggestion of revamping the system cost Merkel a significant lead in the polls. In the end, her party squeaked by with a lead of just 1 percent of the vote, but Merkel had learned an invaluable lesson—the best idea will be worthless if you can't communicate it effectively and give people what they think they want.

After that, Merkel became a master in taking the public's temperature, and basing her politics on the prevailing sentiment. She became obsessed with polling. Before proposing any major shifts in policy, she would first calculate whether the public had her back. In March of 2011, she made a decision that raised eyebrows around the world and opened her up to a raft of criticism from outside the country. After the deadly meltdown of a nuclear power plant in Fukushima, Japan, triggered by a tsunami, she announced that Germany would shut down eight of its nuclear power plants. The decision was a reversal on her previous policy and seemed to make little sense in a country that was already looking to swap its fossil-fuel-burning power plants for wind turbines and solar panels to decarbonize the system. But Germans' fear of nuclear disaster runs deep. Even political debates are fueled not by facts and sage arguments but raw emotion. Tens of thousands of people had marched past the chancellery waving bright yellow flags reading NUCLEAR ENERGY, *nein danke!* after her government had passed legislation reversing a previous decision to shorten the lives of the reactors. Merkel understood full well that a majority of Germans opposed atomic energy, and the meltdown in Fukushima had only further soured sentiment on it, despite its low-carbon footprint. On top of that, her party was already struggling ahead of an election in an important southwestern state against the fiercely antinuclear Greens party. The vote would be held less than a week after the disaster in Japan. Sizing up the situation, Merkel decided to reverse course and ordered her country's nuclear reactors powered down to be thoroughly checked for safety. Eight never went back online and the others were taken off ahead of schedule. Many people thought the decision was driven by emotion, but Merkel had sensed the public mood and understood that she had to be the one to change.

Germany's decision to legalize gay marriage in 2017 again proved Merkel's ability to read the room and give the people what they wanted. That move also took place in an election year, only this time a national vote was pending. Germany, along with the rest of Europe, was still grappling to come to terms with the foreign policy of President Trump. Germany also faced the additional weight of having to integrate the more than 1 million migrants who had arrived in the previous years. In the midst of the upheaval, many Germans were clinging to Merkel as the "safe pair of hands" candidate. But others, especially younger and more liberal-minded Germans, felt it was time to change. After twelve years of the same chancellor, they had had enough. One issue that drove them was gay marriage. At the time Germans could enter into legally recognized civil partnerships, but not enjoy the full benefits of marriage, including the right to adopt. Merkel's conservative party viewed that union as being between a man and a woman, and without her party's support, she could not ordinarily get a bill through parliament. But enough members of the other parties supported it to do so.

During an election event, Merkel was asked about her position on gay marriage. She told the story of a lesbian who had written her an invitation to visit her home, so the chancellor could see how she and her partner provided a loving environment for eight foster children. Although she never made the trip, Merkel said the woman's arguments helped her to reconsider her position. Then almost casually, she proposed freeing lawmakers from the constriction of needing to vote along party lines on the issue and allowing everyone to "vote their conscience" on marriage equality. Within weeks, a bill was drawn up, debated, and with a burst of confetti from a longtime gay lawmaker, the right to same-sex marriage passed the German parliament. The final vote, with 4 abstentions, was 393 in favor and 226—including Merkel—against. Afterward she told reporters that she hadn't changed her position. In her mind, marriage remained the union between a man and a woman. But she understood that by opening the door to marriage equality, she was allowing others to reap the same benefits from change that she once had.

"We often have such a fear of change today and think, 'Oh, if something changes now, who knows if it will be better,'" she told a group of high school students in 2014. "For me, it's such a primal experience that in the grand scheme of things . . . it was a change for the better."[8]

RECOGNIZE WHEN OTHERS NEED
TO CHANGE (AND GIVE THEM A NUDGE)

If Helmut Kohl had not pushed through the agreements with the United States, the Soviet Union, and Germany's European partners, Angela Merkel might never have been able to run for her newly reunited country's first joint parliament—a dream that she formed pretty quickly after entering the East German political scene. Had he not tapped her to serve as his minister for women and youth in the new, unified German government, she would have missed the opportunity to examine and experience the inner workings of power, at a time when so much in her country was up for grabs. Merkel had already established herself as a quick study in her approach to life in the former West German capital of Bonn—the all-German capital from 1990 until 1999—and in the conservative Christian Democratic Union, which by the time of reunification had fully absorbed the small party she had initially joined. Kohl served not only as a political mentor. Without realizing it, he taught Merkel the pitfalls of what can happen to politicians who refuse to see that their time has come to step aside and allow others to take the stage.

By publicly calling out the man who had nurtured her career by insisting that her political party needed a new start if it was to survive, Merkel laid the groundwork for a change that the Christian Democrats still wrestle with to this day. Germans were shocked to see the young woman who until then had mostly caught their attention for her unique background and equally unique fashion style make such a blatant grab at power. But she explained the move as necessary to weed out corruption and restore credibility to the conservative party. She feared that the high-profile slush-fund scandal that had embroiled the conservative party and several of its leading members, not only Kohl, smacked of personal greed and a general disrespect of the public they hoped to serve. It lacked integrity. And if there was one quality that Merkel embodied, with her modest pants and blazers to her insistence on personally popping into the grocery story around the corner from the two-bedroom apartment that she still calls home, it was integrity.

"With Angela Merkel you would never have the notion she is bribable," said one of Germany's most prominent Protestant theologians and a former bishop in Germany's Lutheran Church, Margot Käßmann. "She embodies this attitude of serving."[9]

Serving to Merkel meant meeting the people where they are and upholding the laws of the land, not keeping a secret slush fund. By taking the time during her early years as the party's secretary-general to attend local party meetings and share a few beers with members in halls and locales of the far-flung towns and villages across the country, Merkel had understood what they expected of their leaders. Unless Kohl left the party, she was convinced that its integrity would be damaged for years to come. When he refused to see the need to change, she pointed it out.

ACCEPT THAT SOME PEOPLE CAN'T, OR WON'T, CHANGE

When Germany celebrated the twenty-year anniversary of the fall of the Berlin Wall, former Polish president Lech Walesa, who led union protests against the Communist government in Poland in 1980, setting in motion the wheels of change, was granted the honor of tipping the first in a row of giant dominoes assembled along the path where the barrier had stood. But it was Mikhail Gorbachev, the last leader of the Soviet Union, who earned the loudest shouts. The people of Berlin lined up to greet him with cheers of "Gorbi! Gorbi!" as he arrived in the city for the festivities.

Later that night, a beaming Angela Merkel clutched a wide umbrella against the driving rain and led a group of world leaders on a symbolic crossing through the pillars of the German capital's Brandenburg Gate monument. For years it had stood in the former East Germany, just beyond the Berlin Wall, the ultimate symbol of the city's division. Among the guests were then U.S. secretary of state Hillary Clinton, British prime minister Gordon Brown, French president Nicolas Sarkozy, and Dimitry A. Medvedev, the president of Russia. Once on the other side, Merkel addressed the crowds, recalling the night the Berlin Wall came down as one of the happiest in her life.

That was saying something, considering she had just been returned to office and swiftly formed a new government. In the United States, President Barack Obama shared the same vision of promoting democracy and upholding the multilateral agreements established at the end of World War II that Merkel cherished. At the same time, in Medvedev, she had a Russian president who no longer seemed intent on intimidating her, but appeared to embody a Russia that was willing to engage with the West. Speaking in Berlin on the anniversary, he offered what sounded like an olive branch and a path for cooperation, saying about the Cold War, "We all hope that this period of confrontation has become a thing of the past. Today's transition to a new multipolar world is very important for most countries, for all European countries and the entire world."[10]

That vision of Russia, which Merkel fought to the end of her chancellorship to salvage, could not last. Within less than three years, Vladimir Putin was back in power in Moscow, and the West was back on its guard. From May 2012 until she left office, the Western world came to see Merkel as the one leader who understood Putin. It helped that she could understand everything that he said and even speak with him directly, in his own language. But languages can also be displays of power. When two speakers, one native and one who has learned the language later in life, meet, even if the non-native speaker is highly fluent, the native speaker will always have the upper hand. I know from my own experience speaking German, a language that I learned when I was twenty-two and now speak on a level that is often mistaken for native, that a true native speaker can navigate the subtleties of nuance, humor, and irony quicker and more efficiently. Although Merkel had excelled in Russian at school, she knew that Putin's skills in speaking German exceeded hers in Russian—a gift from the Stasi, as she once joked to a colleague as they stood in the German parliament in 2001 to applaud the Russian leader on a speech he had given to the assembly.

Merkel told her advisers and partners she never had any illusions about the Russian leader. In her eyes, he would forever be an agent of Russia's KGB who willingly collaborated with East Germany's secret police, the Stasi, while her acquisition of the Russian language had been one of curiosity and joy, embracing the literary greats Leo Tolstoy and

Fyodor Dostoyevsky. For years she kept on her desk in the chancellery a small portrait of Catherine the Great, the Russian czarina who was born in the German principality of Anhalt-Zerbst. Putin's relationship to the German language, however, had always been purely transactional.

While she joined the crowds of East Germans flowing into the West to celebrate their freedom at the Berlin Wall's demise, Putin watched the local Stasi boss take his own life as crowds descended on the KGB offices in the East German city of Dresden, where Putin had been stationed. When he sought help from the Soviet military stationed nearby, he was rebuffed. The orders must come from Moscow, he was told, and that night Moscow was silent.[11]

If Merkel saw the events that night as the inspiration that would change her world for the better, Putin took a quite different view. He made clear his interpretation of the events surrounding the collapse of Communism in a speech he gave to Russian lawmakers in 2005, months before Merkel would take her first oath of office as reunited Germany's third democratically elected chancellor, when he said, "The collapse of the Soviet Union was the greatest geopolitical catastrophe of the century."[12]

Over the next sixteen years, they would spend countless hours on the phone and have numerous meetings in person. Early in their relationship, Putin would try to taunt Merkel with scare tactics, such as setting his black Lab loose during a press conference, knowing she was uncomfortable around dogs. After she rallied the European Union to impose sanctions on Russia following Moscow's illegal annexation of Crimea in 2014, he became more brazen, sending an assassin to take out a rival in a park in the heart of Berlin, just a mile from the chancellery where Merkel had her office. But Merkel refused to flinch. She shrugged off his attempts to embarrass her, whether in public, or by setting his hackers on the software systems of the German parliament, exposing their lax security. But she kept meeting him, kept speaking to him.

A fellow European leader expressed surprise at Merkel's willingness to keep meeting the Russian leader, despite the public humiliations. Merkel replied that she had no illusions about Putin. An aide of hers told me that Merkel had recognized immediately that, with Putin, she was dealing with a KGB man, in short, an agent of the Russian security agency, little different from the East German spies her parents had warned her about as a child. By the time they met, the Soviet Union had collapsed, the Cold War had ended, and the world had moved on. But Putin remained stuck in a past that he considered his life's mission to restore. Merkel's greatest miscalculation may have been failing to fully understand just how far he was willing to go to try to do just that. But she knew that ignoring him would only further damage his already bruised ego.

As long as she remained in power, Merkel remained determined to keep Putin engaged—on the telephone, at the negotiating table, at any opportunity she could get. When the coronavirus pandemic hit, sending the world into isolation, Putin was no exception, embodied by the ridiculously long tables that he chose for holding meetings in the waning days of the pandemic. Her words proved prophetic. By the time that Russia was massing troops on the border with Ukraine, Merkel was a lame duck, unable to take the steps she understood would be necessary to try to stop the Russian president from making the one move she had fought throughout her chancellorship to prevent—plunging Europe back into a protracted, bloody war. When the European leader expressed to Merkel her shock that she appeared so willing to let Putin belittle her in public and use his propaganda machine to rile up Germans who sided with the Russian strongman, Merkel admitted she knew what he was up to and why he had to do it. But she took it willingly, she said. Being humiliated by Putin seemed a small price to pay, she replied, if Europe could remain at peace.

Chapter 6

PRACTICE
RESOLUTE PRAGMATISM

Women, I think, tend to have
a certain yearning for efficiency.
—ANGELA MERKEL, 2021

From a global financial crisis to a surge of migrants making their way to
Europe, to a pandemic, and always against the backdrop of the threat of
an ever-warming climate—a trial or upheaval marked each of the four
terms that Angela Merkel spent in office. In a unique way, each tested
her capability and skill as a leader. But her response to each reflected
the resolute pragmatism she brought to such challenges, approaching
them with a deep understanding of the stakes at hand and an unbending
determination to do whatever it took in each case to reach a solution.
Often, Merkel would capitalize on a turning point or unstable time
to enact changes she understood were needed but might otherwise be
difficult to achieve. Sometimes, it was because she lacked the political
support of her conservative party, as was the case involving the phase-
out of nuclear energy. Already in 2010, a majority of Germans wanted
to see Germany go nuclear-free, but not the members of her party. So
she seized upon the fear and uncertainty surrounding the disaster in
Fukushima, Japan, the following year to push her government to speed
up the shuttering of the country's remaining nuclear reactors.

Toward the end of her final term, she realized that the time had come to convince Germans to accept the sharing of debt among the European countries if the Continent was to have any hope of emerging from the lockdowns of the coronavirus pandemic with the least possible economic harm. A known champion of frugality, Merkel had long defended Germany's nationalistic approach to European finances. That meant although the countries shared a currency, each was responsible for its own budget, spending, and debt. But after Germany's partners in Europe published an open letter calling the Germans out for what amounted to their stingy approach—their prosperity was largely thanks to the economic union—she changed tack. In the previous decade, she had sold reluctant Germans on the idea of keeping Greece in the union, although at a painfully heavy price to the Greek people, in the name of democracy and solidarity. This time, it was not one country that faced financial difficulties, it was all of them. The months of economic standstill resulting from the lockdowns aimed at sparing lives by preventing the coronavirus from spreading had left no country unaffected. If the European project that she had fought to preserve was to continue, Germany had to practice the solidarity that Merkel had for years preached.

Once she had made up her mind about a policy, Merkel would set about shifting her messaging. Often she would repeat the same catchphrases over and over; sometimes the shift was more subtle. In the speech she gave to the nation on March 18, 2020, for example, Merkel used the words "Europe" or "European" thirty-nine times, to signal the importance of the whole bloc of nations supporting one another.[1] Two months later, she announced Germany's support for a joint recovery package to help the whole of the EU get back on its feet. Observers celebrated what they deemed Europe's "Hamiltonian moment," in a nod to Alexander Hamilton, the founding father of the U.S. Treasury—and now Broadway musical—fame, whose "dinner table compromise" got Thomas Jefferson and James Madison to agree to consolidate and share the individual debts among the former U.S. colonies.[2] To sell her deal to the reluctant German public, Merkel said the 500-billion-euro recovery fund was a one-off response to the unique postpandemic moment. It was a chance, she said, for Europe to emerge from the crisis stronger than it had gone into it—another of her favorite phrases. Since the collapse of Communism in Europe, Merkel had come to view crises as opportunities.

While each response differed, as did the crises themselves, many of her tactics at handling them remained the same, honed over time. Merkel came into politics already armed with many of her best-known crisis-combating skills. As a scientist, she had won the admiration of her professors and peers for her ability to quickly absorb enormous amounts of information. When she moved to the chancellery, this didn't change. Unlike Margaret Thatcher, who had the pages of her speeches cut to fit into her iconic black leather, top-handled handbags, Merkel chose her handbag large enough to fit a stack of the thick folders stuffed with standard-size sheaves of paper. Her collection of Longchamp Le Pliage bags included models in dark red, orange, and black, which she coordinated with her rainbow of blazers. More important to her than the fashion aspect was the practicality. She believed that every encounter, meeting, or event deserved to be approached with the same level of attention to detail and advance preparation, and that required the right equipment. When Merkel arrived at a meeting or a session of parliament, the first thing she would do was place her bag on the table before her and draw out her stack of folders—and usually her cell phone. Normally, they served more as a backup, as she had already studied their contents. But it was a signal that she meant business and was ready to focus on the task at hand. It was this approach and her ability to rise to the occasion in the face of a challenge that seemed to stymie those around her that earned Merkel the respect of her peers and the nickname the Crisis Chancellor.

BE THE BEST-PREPARED
PERSON IN THE ROOM

The day after she took her oath of office, Angela Merkel traveled to Paris, maintaining a postwar tradition of German chancellors paying a visit to their French counterpart. But instead of returning home to Berlin, Merkel continued her journey to Brussels. There she was greeted by hundreds of staff with shouts of "Angie!" They jostled and waved to catch a glimpse of the leader who from her earliest days in office stressed the importance of maintaining a strong European Union.

That she had turned up in Brussels barely more than twenty-four hours since coming into power was a novelty for German leaders. Traditionally London or Warsaw served as their second stop on an introductory tour. But Merkel knew the European Union faced a critical decision, and she wanted to send a signal that she recognized the importance of the institution and her country's role within it. Sixteen years later, when she left for the final time as chancellor, many people wondered how the EU bloc of nations would function moving ahead as she had made herself such an integral part of its negotiating processes.

During that first trip, the bloc faced tough challenges. Ten new countries, most of them former satellites of the Soviet Union, had joined the EU the previous year. The EU now stretched from Portugal to the Baltic states, which shared a border with Russia, and getting this unwieldy group to agree meant understanding where each one stood and why it held its particular positions. Several weeks after her inaugural visit, Merkel returned to Brussels to attend her first summit, when leaders of the member states gathered to make decisions on financial or foreign policies. That year, in the final weeks of 2005, the EU members faced a ticking clock to end a deadlock over the terms of a new budget. At stake was how many millions, if not billions, of euros each member would pay or receive over the coming five years. An agreement had to be reached by the start of the new year and an earlier attempt to resolve the thorny issue had resulted only in everyone digging in deeper on its position. Italy and Spain didn't want to see funds redirected from their nations to newer members, and the Dutch and the Swedes, among the wealthiest members, wanted to reduce their contributions. Paris and London remained locked in a battle over agricultural subsidies for France and a special rebate for Britain—still an EU member at the time. Untangling the squabbling seemed impossible, and those who had been trying to negotiate an agreement for months were out of ideas on a path forward. None of them expected the neophyte chancellor to make a difference; they hoped only that she might be more pro-European than her predecessor, who had done little to resolve the situation.

Dalia Grybauskaitė knew better. As the commissioner responsible for the EU budget, her job was to work with European leaders, going over details, explaining the finer points of how money was distributed among the members, or the importance of certain portfolios for individual countries. The president of the European Commission, José Manuel Barroso, had organized a dinner during Merkel's inaugural visit to Brussels. He invited Grybauskaitė because he thought it would be helpful to have an expert there to explain the various camps, their interests, disputes, and the overall view of what was at stake. That's not how their meeting went.

The new German chancellor arrived, a collection of folders in hand, but already up to speed on the details of each member country. Instead of asking how much any one of them contributed or received, she peppered the commissioner with questions about who she thought could cede ground on which points. Merkel also wanted to sound out different members' red lines. Grybauskaitė, who would be elected president of Lithuania in 2009, joining Merkel as one of the few female heads of state on the world stage, remembered her surprise at that first time she was confronted with Merkel's brain. "She knew deeply all details of any file pending in the European Commission and any file pending in the European Parliament, and it was just her first week in office,"

Grybauskaitė told me. "It was not just on the level of a head of state, but she knew everything."[3]

Merkel took a similarly thorough approach before her first meeting with President Donald Trump. In the weeks leading up to her trip to Washington, she spent hours watching episodes of his reality TV show, *The Apprentice*. She had her aides find an interview he gave to *Playboy* magazine in 1990, which was being carefully studied on both sides of the Atlantic in an attempt to understand the new U.S. president, and read his book *The Art of the Deal*. While it still wasn't enough to prepare her for Trump's legendary refusal to shake her hand for the photographers, as is protocol at such bilateral meetings, by then she knew enough not to let it bother her. Merkel just shrugged and laughed it off.

But negotiating in Brussels meant knowing more than just one individual's position. By the time she left office, there were twenty-seven members of the EU. Once there, Merkel would put her information to use. Her style was to take individuals aside and probe them with questions. When sessions got heated with anger rising on opposing sides, she would make a joke—often poking fun at herself—to ease the tension. When other leaders would send in an adviser to sit at the table and retreat to their office sofas for a nap, she stayed put, a blanket pulled over her shoulders to ward off the chill of the air conditioner when it grew late. Often she would get up to discuss one-on-one with other leaders, bring two opposed parties together, serving as a mediator between them. Her aim was to use her knowledge to find an agreement that everyone could get behind, however long it took.

As the clock ticked into the early-morning hours of Saturday at her first summit in 2005, Merkel managed to bring the bitterly opposed British prime minister and president of France together, probing, listening, suggesting solutions, going back and forth sounding out points where they could agree. Tony Blair, the actual leader of the negotiations, had gone into the talks skeptical that a deal could be reached. But Merkel also came armed with a proposal that all the older EU countries agree to take a financial hit for the sake of the newer, economically weaker members, which everyone finally agreed to back. Reaching more than just a deal, Europe emerged with a new leader, one whose acumen and dedication to the dream of a Continent united and at peace would shepherd it through the coming decade of financial and humanitarian crises.

"It was the first time I saw that extraordinary capability of [her] just wanting always to be the problem solver,"[4] Blair said afterward. It would not be the last.

LEARN WHERE YOU
SHARE COMMON GROUND

Before Chancellor Merkel flew to Washington for her initial meeting with President George W. Bush—in 1991 she had met his father, whom she revered for his role in paving the way for German reunification—she peppered her U.S. ambassador with questions about the man. It was not only points of policy she wanted to know, but some personal details. What drove him? What were his interests? His values?

It wasn't just data and the documents; preparation for Merkel included delving into an individual's background before a meeting, or surveying a population to get a feel for where they stood on key issues and gaining a sense for potentially unspoken motivating factors. She then used the knowledge to establish common ground between herself and another individual or audience, forming a connection.

With President George W. Bush, she found an in through his faith. After learning that he was deeply Christian, she drew on her experiences growing up as a Lutheran pastor's daughter as an icebreaker. When he showed an interest in the former East Germany, wanting to know about her experiences growing up there, she organized a barbecue for him in her constituency in the eastern state of Mecklenburg–West Pomerania. The roast pig, along with deer and duck, in the village of several hundred inhabitants, in the heart of Germany's most sparsely populated state, served as the closest she could come to re-creating the vastness of his Prairie Chapel Ranch, outside Crawford, Texas. Several years later, President Bush gave her a personal tour of his property, after she and her husband accepted a return invitation for a visit.

When Bush Sr. died in November 2018, Merkel immediately cleared her schedule and arranged to fly to Washington for the funeral. Once there, she reached out to the younger former president Bush directly. Knowing how close he had been to his father, she wanted to offer him and his family her condolences in person. He recalled that gesture of warmth and friendship as a reflection of the genuine, value-driven person that Merkel is and the qualities of principle that she brought to her leadership. He understood, and marveled at, how she had translated that into an extended term in office. "Here's the thing that amazes me—eight years in a democracy is a long time. I know full well, people get tired of you. . . . And Angela Merkel has managed to survive in a pretty tough political environment for more than eight years. And it's pretty amazing when you think about it," he said. "The tenure reflects something, and I think it reflects the German voters' trust. They may not always agree with Angela, but they trust her."[5]

KNOW HOW TO READ THE ROOM

Merkel understood from her earliest political experiences that trust cannot be bought or won, it must be built. It stands on a foundation of careful listening and weighing the options, finding the right time to make a move, and a willingness to put in the work before arriving at any event, whether a press conference or a bilateral meeting with another world leader. From her earliest days in politics, she had found that navigating a crisis with a clear head and calm demeanor engendered confidence from those around you. From her spontaneous appointment as a spokeswoman at the start of her career, to her taking over the conservative party leadership after speaking out against Helmut Kohl, Merkel had a history of using points of great uncertainty or upheaval to move forward, bringing others with her. It was just such a situation that allowed her to cement the trust of the German people on a sunny Sunday afternoon in October 2008.

Europe had been engulfed by the financial crisis triggered by the collapse of Lehman Brothers bank in the United States weeks earlier, and Britain, France, and Italy were looking to Germany to contribute 75 billion euros to a fund that would shore up shaky banks and keep the crisis from engulfing the Continent. Merkel wasn't having it. She had already provided guarantees worth several billions to help German lenders and believed the responsibility should fall to the financial sector, not to the state. Then came news from Germany's central bank that people were withdrawing large amounts of cash from ATMs. They were after 500-euro bills—the largest note in the common European currency. This wasn't just Germans getting ready to head off on a shopping spree over the three-day-long holiday weekend. People were worried about their savings. They were losing faith in the banks.

Her government needed to take action to mitigate the fears and assure people that their savings were safe. If not, the consequences could see panicking Germans bringing down the whole of the eurozone, the group of countries that shared the common European currency. In that moment, Merkel decided to call the press and give a statement, telling Germans the government would back their savings. No matter what. She informed her finance minister, Peer Steinbrück, of her plan. But he balked, worried that if she went it alone, he as finance minister would have to make his own statement about an hour later, which could cause confusion and undermine the entire project. Merkel might have been new in her role as chancellor, but she knew her government had only one chance to get it right. And she had no doubts, the statement had to be clear, concise, and direct. This wasn't a question of competition between herself and her finance minister, it was a matter of demonstrating cohesion and competence as a team. She picked up the phone again and called her finance minister back, telling him they would make a joint appearance.

A small group of reporters—mostly those with cameras—and photographers were called to the Skylobby of the chancellery, a bright open space lined with paintings and soaring windows a half flight down from Merkel's offices. As the bulbs flashed, the pair appeared. The chancellor looked at the clutch of lenses and microphones pushed toward her face, then looked over her shoulder and shifted a step to her left, taking care to position herself before a landscape painting with swirls of dark blue and yellow as a backdrop. Then, turning to the cameras, she looked straight ahead, her blue eyes open wide and her voice steady.

"To all people with savings, we say that your deposits are safe," she said, nodding her head in gentle reassurance. "The German government stands behind them."[6]

The pair took no questions but thanked the reporters and exited the room quickly. The reason? They could not have provided any answers. "We had no legal basis, we had no parliamentary decision, we had nothing," Steinbrück said.[7] The language they had chosen had been deliberately vague and the meeting with the press equally so. But the gamble worked. Although Merkel would later have to change course and bail out Germany's banks with a multibillion-euro fund, on that day Germans left their cash in the banks. She had shown that she understood what people needed to hear to feel confident in their savings and responded.

DECIDE ON YOUR GOAL AND REMAIN COMMITTED TO ACHIEVING IT

In summer 2012, Greece—again—found itself teetering on the brink of insolvency, engulfed by debt that it could not repay. Angela Merkel found herself in the midst of a game of brinkmanship. By that point, the cycle had been going on for nearly three years.

Talk of Greece's leaving the shared European currency, making a
"Greek exit," or "Grexit," was rife in Berlin. Merkel's advisers were giving
her conflicting advice over whether it would cost Germany more to keep
the Greeks or to let them crash out. The decision was not hers alone, but
Germany's economic power meant that without approval from Berlin, a
bailout or other financial assistance would not happen. German media
had a field day with reports of how wealthy Greeks used military tarps
to cover their backyard swimming pools as a vivid example of the extent
people in Greece would go to avoid paying taxes. The images helped feed
local stereotypes of Greeks as lazy spendthrifts who worked fewer hours
and retired earlier than Germans did. Outrage at the idea that German
taxpayers' euros could be spent to help cover Greek debt grew. Many
Germans expected their chancellor to hold firm to the strict terms of demanded reforms from Greece in exchange for a multibillion-euro bailout
package, its second in as many years, even as the United States and other
Western partners begged Germany to cut the Greeks some slack in the
name of European solidarity.

For Merkel, the question of what to do with Greece went beyond the
financial. At that point, the European Union and its shared currency
had been endeavors embraced and underwritten by her predecessors in
office. Did she, who had embraced the chance at democracy handed
her by history, really want to be the woman who opened the door for
a member to quit the seventeen-nation currency when she could have
prevented it? Worse, what if such a move rattled political faith in the
European project, causing the construct that she credited with bringing peace and prosperity to Germany and the Continent to collapse?
Two years earlier, as the extent of the economic problems facing Greece
had come to light, she had made up her mind where she stood on the
issue. "The monetary union is a community of fate. It is therefore a
matter of nothing more and nothing less than preserving and proving
the European idea," she said. "This is our historic task, because if the
euro fails, Europe fails."[8]

That phrase became Merkel's mantra, repeated over and over, whether in parliament, at political rallies, or in speeches to the country's various business associations. In her life as a scientist, Merkel had learned that when presenting information to her peers, nobody was interested in anything but your latest discovery. Once you had informed them, they were good and did not want to hear of it again. As a politician, she found the need to repeat a political message time and again—even several times within the same speech—to ensure it stuck, strange and difficult. By the time the debt crisis hit Europe, she not only knew the drill, but had internalized its importance.

Over those years she repeated the phrase "If the euro fails, then Europe fails" like a mantra at every possible opportunity. It popped up in her speeches to business and industry associations and statements to the press so often that we journalists stopped quoting it. That didn't stop her. For Merkel knew by then that if one country crashed out of the shared currency, it could weaken its value and undermine the whole of the European project. In those years, before the British voted to leave the bloc, the European Union appeared fraught and fragile. Each summit became an all-night marathon of negotiations that depended on Merkel's mediation skills to reach resolution.

At the same time, she remained convinced that without addressing the problem of the euro crisis at its root, namely the budgetary flaws that had led to overspending—in short, a flaunting of the rules—there would be no bailout big enough to ensure the euro's long-term stability. Years before the Berlin Wall collapsed, Merkel had been convinced that East Germany's economy, riddled with corruption and weakened by inaction, could not survive. In 1991, she made her publishing debut in a leading Berlin daily, arguing for the need to consolidate East Germany's economy along the lines of the free-market system that had been implemented in West Germany after World War II. Only through reform of its economy, she argued, would society be able to recover.

Her treatise included a healthy dose of the Protestant work ethic she had been raised on, which also came into play in her approach to solving the debt crisis in Europe. If Germany was going to help bail out other eurozone countries, then in exchange they would have to tighten their spending and enact painful measures that would ensure their financial systems were more robust in the end.

But Europe's first attempt to impose budget cuts on Greece in exchange for financial help had led to job losses and tax hikes that left many burning wood to heat their homes and lining up at food pantries to feed their families. Frustrated Greeks took to the streets that spring and summer in a fiery outburst of anger. While some groups set buildings alight, throwing homemade bombs and clashing with riot police, tens of thousands of equally angry but more peaceful people staged general strikes, gathering on the steps of the Greek parliamentary building to vent. The main target of their ire was Merkel. They waved images of her dressed as a Nazi in a brown shirt and Hitler's toothbrush mustache, or as a dominatrix with her leather boot planted firmly on a map of southern Europe, and shouted slogans against German domination.

France, Britain, and the United States were all calling on Merkel to assuage the situation, either by easing up on her demands for deeper budget cuts from the Greeks, or by agreeing to have Germany take on shared debt. Her polling told her that both moves lacked support at home.

A year earlier, at the Group of 20 summit in Cannes, Merkel had found herself in a conference room with the American and French presidents, who were pressuring her to agree to increase the eurozone's crisis-fighting cash reserves. President Obama and Nicolas Sarkozy of France had devised a way that it could happen without calling on the European Central Bank to print money. Such a move seemed an obvious response to the crisis at the time. But both knew the specter of hyperinflation, such as that which had weakened Germany's fledgling democracy after World War I, leaving it vulnerable to a nationalist takeover by Adolf Hitler, still spooked the Germans. They would never support it. As a work-around, Obama and Sarkozy had devised a financial tool that did not involve the European Central Bank, but did require approval from Germany's central bank, the Bundesbank. After a flurry of phone calls back and forth with the bank's leader in Frankfurt, he refused to agree.

Ever in search of a compromise, Merkel suggested that other European countries could go ahead with the plan, while Germany sat it out. Obama pushed back, insisting that without the backing of Europe's largest economy, the markets wouldn't be convinced and the whole scheme would collapse. Merkel stood firm, insisting that France and the United States, as former Allied powers, had only themselves to blame for Germany's complex, decentralized system of government. After all they, the Allies, had set it up with layers of checks and balances to specifically prevent any one individual from usurping too much power.

They weren't interested in a history lesson. Instead, they pressed harder, effectively urging Merkel to override her central banker. The chancellor snapped. "That is not fair," she cried, emotion rising in her voice, tears welling up in her eyes. "I cannot decide in lieu of the Bundesbank. I cannot do that."[9]

Stunned that they had pushed the woman known across Europe and around the world for her cool head and her unflappable staying power in a negotiation to the breaking point, Obama and Sarkozy backed off. The deal never came to pass. On the way out of the meeting, President Obama reached over and threw his arm around Merkel, trying to make things right. The White House photographer captured the moment, where Obama is looking down with a softened gaze at the chancellor, who tried to force a smile in return, but appeared more than ready to escape the whole situation, especially the embrace.

Eventually, the European Central Bank promised free unlimited support for indebted countries, including Greece, restoring trust in the euro and calming financial markets. But many Germans and, especially, Greeks remained unsatisfied. When Merkel visited Athens in October 2012 in what she called a gesture of solidarity—Merkel fashion watchers noted, however, that she donned the same light green blazer that she had worn the night that Germany defeated Greece 4–2 during the European soccer championship that June—the people of Greece made sure the chancellor felt their anger and dismay at the austerity measures that had left many without incomes or jobs.

As her motorcade sped from the airport to the center of Athens, a mob broke through the cordons of riot police, pelting her black sedan with bottles. Outside the parliament building, she was met by tens of thousands of protesters who had poured into the streets, some brandishing a giant banner reading MERKEL RAUS, German for "Merkel get out." Others waved pictures of her dressed in the drab brown shirts of the Nazi uniform, or with her image doctored to show her hair slicked back and a toothbrush mustache bristling beneath her nose. The message was unmistakable: in the eyes of the Greeks, the demands she had made and continued to make of them were equivalent to the atrocities committed in Greece and across Europe by Adolf Hitler. Merkel took it all in. Years later, she would let on how painful it had been to see the work she had intended to help people be thrown back in her face, to be mocked and blamed for their suffering. A politician can't be a snowflake. She smiled and insisted during a press conference that she was there not to lecture, but to learn firsthand about people's suffering, in hopes of helping to provide workable answers. "I am not here to be a teacher," she said. "I am here to be informed."[10]

Chapter 7

PROTECT YOUR PRIVATE LIFE

I have always made sure that there were boundaries,
that certain parts of my life were off-limits.

—ANGELA MERKEL, 2021

Days after she had been grilled in the German parliament over rising rents and compensation for health-care workers, then appeared bleary-eyed and struggling not to slur her speech at an early-morning news conference following an all-night crisis meeting over Great Britain's request to extend its plan for exiting the European Union, Angela Merkel buried her mother.

The few reporters who showed up for Herlind Kasner's funeral kept a respectful distance from the baroque church in central Templin, where Merkel's father had preached in Angela's youth. Merkel, her husband, siblings, and their families entered through a side door shrouded by a tarp strung up to prevent the photographers' long lenses from prying. After the service, everyone respected the family's decision that only its closest members would gather at the cemetery for a private burial. Afterward, they headed to a tiny, half-timbered church several miles outside town on a hill miles from the nearest village. Merkel's father had helped save the chapel, built by Protestant pilgrims in the seventeenth century, from ruin after the collapse of the Communist system. It remained a special and symbolic place for the Kasner siblings. Surrounded by the thick trunks of ancient linden trees, it was also about as isolated a property as could be found, even in the sparsely populated, rolling landscape that unfolds around the lakes in the region, where Merkel and her husband have had a summer home for decades.

Years later, speaking about the challenge of managing grief while in the public eye, Merkel recalled juggling the crushing loss of her mother at a time when her packed schedule and duties as chancellor had demanded her full attention. Gripping a microphone in her left hand, she stiffly drew four corners in the air with her right hand, as if showing how she had built her own special wall around her life outside politics. It served not to prevent people from leaving, but to protect herself, her sanity, by keeping them out. "You have to build your own room," she said. "I didn't let in anyone who didn't belong there and that worked."[1]

Merkel came to power at the same time as reality TV began to take off. Before long, social media sites appeared, allowing strangers to take part in the most intimate parts of an individual's life. But Merkel remained immune to oversharing. Instead, she handed out details of her private life like tantalizing sweet delicacies, giving up only so much about what she planted in the garden at her weekend house, how she handled the potatoes in her legendary soup—smashed by hand, not pureed, to leave some toothsome chunks—and how she spent her free time.

Anyone who worked with the chancellor or was allowed into her closest circle as a friend quickly learned that the price for access was discretion. Even individuals invited for a personal meeting with the chancellor were informed to keep the details of what had passed between them to themselves. A betrayal of her trust meant being swiftly shut out. Early in her political career, Merkel decided to apply the same skepticism of the outside world that she had been taught growing up in a system awash with government spies. She never shook her wariness of letting anyone know too much about what went on at her home, or in her mind. This allowed her to create a personal bubble around her innermost sanctum where she could retreat from the daily stresses of leading her country and draw strength from the peace she found there.

CONTROL YOUR IMAGE,
EVEN IN THE SUPERMARKET

With the advent of smart phones came the explosion of images, including the selfie. Merkel had taken to cell phones early on in her career, fascinated by the handheld computers that had more power than the IBM she had used to process data toward the end of her career as a physicist at the Academy of Sciences. Yet for all that Merkel could be seen during drawn-out sessions in parliament cell phone in hand, sending off text messages—up to fifty per day—she left the photography to the many professionals who surrounded and accompanied her.

Even in the region where she grew up, where many people either knew her or her family personally, she made few exceptions. Before a birthday party she was holding in the region, the staff were given strict instructions not to speak to the press or reveal any details about what went on at the event. Singers who were engaged to perform at the event received an extensive briefing to drill into them the necessity of treating the chancellor as they would any friend of their mother's who happened to be celebrating—act normal around her, don't stare, and do not ask for a selfie. Only for a calculated good reason would Merkel break that rule.

After Germany won the soccer World Cup in Rio de Janeiro in 2014, she smiled demurely behind the golden trophy, as the team's feel-good player, a beaming Lukas Podolski, stretched out his arm to take the photo. The forward later auctioned off a signed print of the selfie to raise 5,000 euros for charity. The following year, as Merkel toured the shelters for some of the hundreds of thousands of people who had arrived as refugees in Germany, she was mobbed by people wanting to grab a personal pic with the woman they credited with giving them a new lease on life. Many of them felt personally indebted to the chancellor, who allowed several of the mostly young Syrian men to snap selfies with her. The images that filled social media and newspaper pages that year were part of a concerted effort to raise acceptance among those Germans who were reluctant to welcome the new arrivals by giving them a human face. It also sent the message to the growing number of nationalists across the country that she stood by her decision to allow the refugees into the country.

That photographic generosity does not apply to fellow customers in the supermarket. Known to personally show up in the store around the corner from her Berlin apartment, Merkel approaches her shopping with the same seriousness as a matter of state. Anyone who happens to glance across the aisle and see Merkel picking up a bottle of wine, some cold cuts, cheese, or toilet paper—during the pandemic when Germans were hoarding the stuff, the chancellor earned widespread respect for having only one pack in her shopping cart—should not dare to ask for a selfie. Unlike the Obamas, who decided in 2017 they would turn down selfie requests in hopes of directly engaging more with people instead of just grabbing a photo, Merkel rooted her rule in practicality. "When I go shopping, I don't allow any selfies, because I otherwise get discombobulated, and the customers do, too," she once explained. "I have put the wrong items in my shopping cart and so have they."[2]

By the end of her second term in office, Merkel had convinced even the country's most powerful tabloids that photos of her and her family while on vacation were off-limits. When the most widely read paper, *Bild*, published photos in 2013 of the chancellor offering her hand to the child of one of her step-grandchildren, her spokesmen chided the press for publishing images that had not been authorized by Merkel.

"You can be sure that they were not published with the approval of the German chancellor," said one of Merkel's spokesmen days after they appeared on the covers of tabloids and women's magazines alike. "You can imagine that it's not always relaxing when you're on vacation somewhere and you have the feeling that a lens is peeking out from every corner."[3] He exhorted the Berlin press corps to consider their "responsibility" in how they should handle the images, praising those outlets that had chosen to obscure the faces of the children to protect their privacy. With little debate over whether Merkel's draconian defense of her private sphere conflicted with the laws of press freedom, which do not grant public figures the same level of control over their personal images as private individuals, the photos all but disappeared from the internet. The following year when the British tabloids published pictures of Merkel in a black one-piece bathing suit, their German counterparts refused to print them, instead publishing finger-wagging stories asking, "Is that really necessary?"[4] This nearly impenetrable wall of privacy often baffled reporters from other countries. In an age when U.S. politicians used their social media pages to directly reach out to constituents, Merkel's reserve came across as aloof and arcane. But beyond allowing her to create a protective world where she could be a human first and a politician second, this refusal to overshare created an aura about her that served as its own power. "She's so mysterious," the comedian Tracey Ullman, known for her sketches of Merkel on her comedy show, gushed to me. "She has a mystique, which is wonderful."[5]

KEEPING PRIVACY IN THE FAMILY

If Merkel rewrote the rule book on privacy, her husband, Joachim Sauer, a professor of quantum chemistry, took it to the next level. Sauer—whose name translates in English to "sour" or "angry"—made no secret about his aversion to public life. From the moment that his wife announced her candidacy for the chancellorship in 2005, he rebuffed journalists, refusing to give any interviews that were not about his research. He avoided campaign events and public events or rallies. In Germany, politicians' spouses and families generally play a much smaller role in campaigns and in public life in general. Family photos are rare and few politicians even involve their spouses in their campaigns. Sauer took that to the next level. Throughout Merkel's chancellorship, Sauer made himself so scarce, he became known among the Berlin press corps as the Phantom of the Opera—a play not only on the mysterious, masked hero of Andrew Lloyd Webber's Broadway musical of the same name, but also because the only event where he could more or less be relied on to show up at his wife's side was at the gala opening night of the Bayreuth Festival of Richard Wagner's operas every July. From the Bavarian village, the pair would head off on their summer vacation.

Merkel shared a love of opera with her husband, who was said to be her closest adviser, although she has confessed to enjoying evenings when they could discuss something other than politics. Otherwise the debates and discussions from her work would bleed into what was supposed to be her time off at home. "That can be unbelievably stressful," she said. "On most evenings, I look forward to a lack of politics."[6]

Their marriage is their second for both Merkel and Sauer. She was already divorced when they met at the Academy of Sciences in the former East Germany. By the time she had become minister for women and youth in the early 1990s, they had moved in together without giving the matter much thought. Yet within her conservative party, at the time still heavily influenced by the Roman Catholic Church and its deeply conservative definition of marriage, many felt uncomfortable with the increasingly influential young minister, who as far as they were concerned was living in sin. Merkel met their concerns head-on, speaking openly in her early interviews about her decision to leave her first husband and how leaving an unhappy union to find one that brings fulfillment fit into her definition of conservative. Not everyone was pleased. "It was not understood why I spoke so often about my divorce," she said, adding that she wasn't trying to champion the idea. "My intention was just to acknowledge that defeat is part of life."[7]

When she became minister for women and youth in 1991, one of the Catholic Church's most powerful figures, the cardinal of Cologne, publicly criticized Merkel for living together with a man who was not her husband.[8] She brushed it off at first. But as she rose through the party ranks and began positioning herself for a run to be its leader, she changed her mind about marriage and staying silent. Realizing that, in this case, allowing the public in on her personal life—safely after the fact—could be politically useful. In late December 1998, careful readers of the announcements in the *Frankfurter Allgemeine Zeitung* found a small, typed announcement in the newspaper's back pages. It read, simply, "We married, Angela Merkel and Joachim Sauer."

Merkel and Joachim epitomize the egalitarian union. He had two sons from his previous marriage. Years earlier, Merkel had made peace with the idea that she did not feel that raising a family was compatible with how she practiced politics. Having children "would mean that I would have to give up politics," she said in 1991.[9] Both she and Sauer respected the other's independent pursuit of their careers, although in ways different from how the world around them expected. While he largely declined to play the part of a traditional "first husband," Merkel did not host dinner parties or private gatherings for her husband's peers at the Humboldt University, where he taught, as is traditionally expected from the wife of a professor in Germany. "Of course, how we share roles is relatively unusual," she said, acknowledging that if she had more time to play the role of traditional housewife, "We would certainly have more guests."[10]

She then reflected that "a very busy person" is expected to have a partner at home "who uses all their energy to support the other's well-being and career." Then without specifying which partner she might be referring to in her own marriage, she simply acknowledged, "We can't offer that."

What her husband could and did offer her, however, was the quiet advice she occasionally indicated took place between them. He served as a sounding board at home and in public, a stoic figure who seemed comfortable allowing his wife to take the spotlight. He withstood the constant chatter in the supermarket tabloids about alleged affairs and an impending separation (which as of publication has not yet happened). Although he made himself scarce, preferring to spend his time in his chemistry lab at the Humboldt University, when it really mattered, Sauer would don his tux and appear alongside his wife. Especially on state visits with U.S. leaders. He appeared beside Laura Bush at the pig roast Merkel threw for President George W. Bush and made his way to Washington, DC, from a conference he had been attending in the Midwest in 2011 just in time to see President Obama drape the Presidential Medal of Freedom around his wife's neck. Unaccustomed to Sauer's accompanying her on such visits, in her excitement she jumped out of her limousine and raced toward the stairs of the White House before turning back to wait for him to catch up.

Only when political affairs dovetailed with his own profession would she draw him into service. In 2014, when professors from the Kharkiv National University in Ukraine reached out to their colleagues in Berlin with concerns about being cut from international exchanges after Russia's invasion and annexation of Crimea in 2014, Merkel quietly delegated the issue to her husband. He used his position on a committee at the Humboldt University to ensure German-Ukraine academic ties remained intact.[11]

At home in their Berlin apartment, on the top floor of a prewar building that looks across a canal to the Pergamon Museum on Berlin's Museum Island, they share household duties, with the help of a housekeeper. Although they have lived in the place since 1997, only PROF. SAUER is marked on the doorbell, along with the names GANZ, SCHÖN, and LUSTIG—which roughly translate to "really, quite funny," for places that have been left empty for security reasons, after other renters have died off or moved out. A police detail regularly guards the building, keeping an eye on the knots of tourists who come in hopes of catching a glimpse of the famous inhabitant coming or going.

While Sauer takes on the main responsibilities of weekly shopping and laundry, Merkel said that cooking remained largely her domain.[12] Standard German dishes are among her favorites, including the pounded beef fillets smeared with mustard then wrapped around a pickle and braised in red wine and vegetable broth known as roulade, or kale sautéed in pork fat and served with sausages. Baking, especially her mother's apple cake, or a plain cake topped with streusel, is one of Merkel's hobbies on weekends spent at home. She also learned to use the discussion of cakes and recipes as a way to connect with voters, especially during election campaigns. While she lacked the time to bake in 1992, her second year as minister for women and youth, an election and a new appointment as minister for the environment two years later meant that she was able to spend more time at home and succeeded in baking two plum cakes.

But Merkel's most legendary dish would remain her version of a German staple that each region tweaks to give its own local stamp. "Nobody in the world can make potato soup as I do," she declared in 1992. "I've stopped trying to find someone."[13] Her remark sparked the legend of the chancellor's potato soup. Over the course of her chancellorship, constituents wrote to the chancellery to ask her to reveal her secret recipe, and women's magazines tantalized readers with write-ups about the typical makeup of the dish in the northeastern region where Merkel grew up, calling it "potato soup, chancellor-style." Before she announced her plans to write a political biography to set the record straight on her position on different points of policy, Germans joked that they hoped her memoirs would include her secret recipe. The closest she came was during her final election campaign in 2017, when she revealed the technique that she believed held the secret for its success. "I always puree the potatoes by hand with a potato masher and not with a machine. That way some pieces are always left behind in the soup."[14]

Merkel's potato soup became a symbol of her homelife, one she doled out in anecdotes that left the public always hungry for more. When she announced that she was writing her political memoirs, an employee at a bookshop wondered whether it would include a detailed recipe of her signature dish, the ultimate reveal of her personal life.

RECRUIT ALLIES TO
PROTECT YOUR PRIVACY

When Angela Merkel would show up in the Italian Alps for her summer vacation, word went out to the local photographers to stay well away from the famous guest. Reinhold Messner, one of the world's leading mountaineers, who looked forward to accompanying the chancellor on climbs through the South Tyrolean Alps, would argue that the region's reputation rested on its ability to serve as a retreat, especially to visitors normally in the public eye. Every year a few photos would leak out to the German or British tabloids, but never enough to leave Merkel feeling that she couldn't disconnect and enjoy herself. Messner said she liked to climb up the narrow alpine trails, charging ahead of the group, relishing the feeling of being alone. Finding solitude while in office could prove more challenging than the daily tasks, but by setting the unspoken rule at the outset that her private life was to remain just that, she found allies in protecting that space.

The residents around her weekend home, in the sparsely populated Uckermark district of Brandenburg, about two hours north of Berlin, knew to respect the chancellor's desire for privacy. There she could shop at the local farmers' market or head down through the woods for a swim in the lake without being disturbed. Granted, her bodyguards made sure that anyone who didn't know the privacy drill learned it quickly, but most people were accustomed to Merkel's presence and would simply nod her way in respectful acknowledgment, then go on about their business. She and Sauer had bought the modest two-story home in Hohenwalde, in English literally translated as "high woods," early on in their relationship.

The village perfectly fits Merkel's definition of solitude, "so still that you can hear the breaking of wood, the chirping of birds, and the jumping of fish."[15] It is so small that it lacks even one of the standard trademarks of rural Germany, a church, a bar, and a bakery, and is reachable only by a road of bumpy cobblestones dating back to the days of horse-drawn carriages. A bridle path runs along the back of her fenced-in garden, where she grows the potatoes for her soup, tomatoes, and beans—but no cauliflower, because she said it requires more attention that her erratic schedule would allow, and it attracts too many snails. Once she became chancellor, the simple wooden-lattice fence that had guarded the property was replaced by a sturdier, metal privacy wall. A home across the street was acquired to house the police who accompany her and shoo away anyone approaching the house, requesting they delete any pictures on their cell phones.[16]

People in her former constituency are even more protective. Women from the local chapter of her political party in the northern coastal city of Stralsund who would regularly join her for coffee would laugh and gush about the chancellor's warmth and humor. Pressed for details or anecdotes of the meetings, which took place regularly over the sixteen years that Merkel represented the region in parliament—chancellors are also regularly elected members of the assembly—they demurred. Here, too, the rules of maintaining the chancellor's privacy prevailed. So much so that in the first six weeks after she left office, Merkel chose to spend them in her former constituency on the Baltic Sea coast. The region is known for its stoic people, and it was winter, so she could pull a hood over her head. But even when she was spotted, no one snapped an image of her on a phone and sent it to the tabloids for money or posted it on social media for fame. Merkel had, after all, been their chancellor. For sixteen years she had fought to improve the infrastructure in their region, to find funding for a museum, and to help build up tourism. In return, they respected her right to walk the windswept beach, alone in her thoughts, or listening to *Macbeth*.

Chapter 8

LEADING AS A SCIENTIST

*I believe in the power of enlightenment. The fact that
Europe is where it is today is thanks to the Enlightenment
and the belief that there are scientific findings that are
real and that it is better to stick to them.*

—ANGELA MERKEL, 2020

Merkel loved languages and dreamed of using her award-winning skills in Russian to become a translator or a teacher. She would later impress her staff at the Ministry for the Environment in Bonn when they first heard her speak English more fluently than her West German predecessor. (As chancellor she would rarely speak English in public, although it was the main language she used in friendly exchanges with many of her colleagues.) But studying liberal arts at an East German university would have meant accepting and being willing to propagate the Communist worldview that she had been raised to question.

Under the East German school system, a student needed a teacher's recommendation to enter university, and Merkel's agreed to endorse her as a prospective student of physics. At nineteen, Merkel left Templin for Leipzig University. She would later train as a quantum chemist, carrying out research in statistical and physical chemistry at the Central Institute of Isotope and Radiation Research of the East German state Academy of Sciences. Her dissertation, "Investigation of the Mechanism of Decay Reactions with Single Bond Breaking and Calculation of Their Rate Constants Based on Quantum Chemical and Statistical Methods," earned her the highest possible grade on her doctorate in 1986. On an additionally required thesis to prove sufficient understanding of Marxist-Leninist theory, she earned only the equivalent of a "sufficient," a grade that she proudly wore as proof of her skepticism of the Communist system.

Merkel said that she wanted to understand Einstein's theory of relativity, to explore the thoughts of the people around Robert Oppenheimer, the American theoretical physicist who is credited with being one of the fathers of the atomic bomb.[1] She also found comfort in the laws and theories of the natural sciences. Proven over time and agreed upon as undeniable truths, they stood as a counterbalance to the political world, dominated by the state propaganda machine aimed at pumping out an ideology to shore up a system that she had come as a teenager to realize was inefficient and believed was doomed to fail.[2]

That belief in science would carry over to her life in politics, influencing and informing her rational, fact-based approach to the job of chancellor. When she arrived in Bonn in the first government of reunified Germany, she applied her scientific approach to understanding how to find her place in the power system, which was largely foreign to her. Unlike most of her peers in the conservative party, most of whom had studied law and made their way up through the youth wing of the Christian Democrats, she had to build her networks from the ground up and absorb a tremendous amount of new information about the workings of the government. Applying the same deliberative approach of gathering the facts, analyzing a problem, and weighing the possible outcomes before making a decision that she had learned as a scientist, Merkel carved out a place for herself within her party and later governments. Her understanding of science helped her to play a leading role in galvanizing power around the need for a global answer to climate change, and her ability to clearly explain complicated scientific concepts helped her country to keep people from dying in large numbers during the coronavirus pandemic—and made her into a social media sensation.

It wasn't just that she trusted the doctors and scientists warning that the consequences of allowing life to continue as normal could cost thousands of lives, but also that she understood the reasons behind their thinking. While the United States politicized the debates surrounding lockdowns and masks, with the president undermining the country's top health official, Merkel conferred with Germany's leading virologists and public health officials, using the information they gave her to inform her decisions. When she addressed the public, warning of the dangers in allowing the virus to spread unchecked, she came across as a high school science teacher, one who would help you through the confusion of chemistry to make sure you got the grade you needed. Germans may not all have agreed with the decisions she took, but no one questioned whether she knew what she was talking about.

EXPAND WHAT YOU KNOW

A career as a physicist in East Germany held another attraction for Merkel: science was one of the few professions allowed and even encouraged through its research and publication of its findings to maintain contacts beyond East Germany's borders—even in the West. From an early age, Merkel had learned to look for the spaces within the limitations imposed by the political system around her. Merkel took advantage of this ability to travel, spending time in the Soviet Union, and Czechoslovakia, where she carried out research for her dissertation. Rudolf Zahradník, the professor of chemical physics who worked with her in Prague, recalled her ability to juggle several projects at once without losing her composure or competency. "Even when she was doing three jobs at the same time, she seemed calm," he said years later. Her decision to move into politics had not changed this, he said, describing the chancellor as a scientific phenomenon. "She is what in physics is called constancy of motion. Her character and human characteristics do not change."[3]

By the time that Merkel became Germany's minister for the environment in 1994, she relished the opportunity to explore the international
stage. The portfolio's issues of storing nuclear waste or the possible causes
of climate change, instead of debating West German feminism, felt like a
homecoming to her scientific mind. In 1995, she hosted a global conference on climate change that her predecessor had been able to schedule at
Berlin years earlier, never dreaming he would no longer be in office when
it was held. Suddenly Merkel found herself on the global stage, facing a
deadlock over a politically charged topic, but one that she understood as
a chance for her country to take the lead. First, however, she had to get
all the players lined up.

The night before the conference ended, Merkel was spent. A grueling
schedule combined with a lack of sleep came out in tears of exhaustion.
She considered forgoing a deal and admitting defeat. But her closest
adviser—who would go on to accompany Merkel through sixteen years
in the chancellery and remain on her staff even after she left politics—
wasn't having it. "Now you pull yourself together!" she barked at the
minister. Merkel obeyed.[4] The next day, overlooking an attempt by Saudi
Arabia to derail the consensus at the last minute, Merkel brought down
the gavel, ushering in the global climate movement.

Tackling climate change became a key point in Merkel's first term
in office. But given her conservative party's role as the political home
of Germany's powerful—and often dirty—industries, she found herself
over the years giving in to their demands. German automakers, who provide more than half a million jobs in the country, insisted Merkel water
down attempts by the European Union to limit vehicle emissions in
2018. She went along with it. The longer she stayed in office, the weaker
her efforts to expand renewable energy became. After deciding to phase
out nuclear power in 2011, she turned to affordable, abundant natural
gas piped into Germany from Russia. She called it a "bridge" fuel, arguing that it emitted lower levels of carbon dioxide, which contributed to
warming the earth to dangerous levels. Until Germany could build up its

wind and solar power resources, the gas would keep factories humming, homes warm, and lights burning.

By her fourth term in office, Merkel's reputation as the "climate chancellor" had worn off. In 2019, tens of thousands of students and children in Germany had joined the teenaged Swedish activist Greta Thunberg in staging weekly "strikes," skipping school on Fridays to instead protest for climate justice as part of the Fridays for Future movement. Thunberg, who met Merkel at the United Nations in 2019 and at the chancellery the following year, criticized the chancellor for failing to use her position to do more to save the planet, insisting, "If she would have stepped up and taken responsibility, that could have had everlasting consequences and that could have changed the whole global narrative on the climate emergency."[5]

These harsh words from Thunberg and her supporters stung. Combating climate change lay at the heart of what Merkel saw as her mission. Early in her first term in office, she had expended her political capital, in late-night negotiations over several bottles of wine, convincing President George W. Bush, an oilman who helped to usher in the age of fracking, to agree to take part in climate negotiations led by the United Nations. That 2007 deal, seen at the time as the narrowest of victories, gave momentum to the movement that would culminate eight years later in the Paris Agreement, the world's first legally binding agreement to limit carbon emissions. In many ways, pushing her peers on the international stage to support the crusade against climate change was easier than taking on the powerful lobbies within her own country and government, where the automobile and chemicals industries provided solid, well-paying jobs for more than 1 million people. Convincing them to cut their emissions required a constant balance between standing behind her ideals and risking key political backing and voters.

The most bitter reminder that her climate policies had fallen short came in her final year in office, when Germany's highest court ruled in favor of a group of young Germans who had sued Merkel's government for failing to protect the climate for future generations. The court ordered the government to revise and expand a 2019 law aimed at reducing the country's carbon footprint. The law was rewritten, but it proved a bitter reminder to Merkel that despite working tirelessly since 1994 to push her country ahead in the fight against climate change, she had failed in the eyes of her country's youth. Of all the crises she had to battle, from the financial to the humanitarian, it was the issue easiest to push aside, its threat seemingly always years away. But if the developments on the ground during her time in office fell short of even her own expectations, Merkel never let the world forget that climate change was a pressing issue. She kept it on the agenda of every multilateral meeting she hosted and especially pushed the United States to acknowledge the reality of a warming climate. If Greta Thunberg could stand before the United Nations and scold world leaders for their inaction, it was largely thanks to Merkel and her efforts to maintain the political dialogue around the issue on the international stage.

RELY ON FACTS, NOT EMOTION

As the coronavirus pandemic wore on into late 2020, even Germans who had largely followed Merkel's guidelines on social distancing and masking up were growing weary of the ordeal. Frustration over limited open hours on shops, no out-of-home entertainment, and the threat of curtailed Christmas celebrations led ever more people to embrace conspiracy theories. They flooded the streets to protest the lockdowns and threatened to undermine the progress made on slowing the spread of the virus. Merkel knew people in Germany had had enough of sitting isolated in their homes. She also knew the country's hospitals were stretched to their limits. She knew that letting people gather with their families could cost more lives. So she tried a tactic she had until that point avoided throughout her political career. Standing before parliament, she raised her voice and pressed her hands together, carefully enunciating every sentence; she became emotional.

Unlike President Trump, who could whip a room into a frenzy, or President Obama, who could inspire people with his soaring rhetoric, Merkel was never a great speaker. But she knew her strength lay in her ability to explain complicated topics in a way that made them accessible to people. And in the weeks before Christmas in 2020, she knew that would not be enough to convince people to go along with the science. Years before Kellyanne Conway had sought to defend President Trump's spokesman for lying to the public about the number of people who attended his inauguration in January 2017, Merkel had already understood the siren song that simple explanations could have over people fueled by anger or insecurity. She had seen emotion take the upper hand in the public narrative in the months that followed her decision to leave the borders open, allowing hundreds of thousands of illegal migrants into the country. Her reputation suffered and it cost her party a local election. As the results of the ballot rolled in, Merkel gave in to her own feelings. In an address to her party, she made clear she understood that in a "post-factual" time people were placing more emphasis on their feelings than on the facts that she cherished and had long relied upon to make sense of her own life and of the country that she now led.

"And the feelings of some people go like this: I am driving our country into over-foreignization, Germany will soon be unrecognizable," Merkel started. "Now, it would be illogical to counter this with facts, even if I—you know me well enough for that—could recite them off the top of my head."

Then to prove her point that emotion, unlike facts, could be bent to reflect the version of reality sought by any given individual, she added her own: "I want to counter this with a feeling. I feel absolutely certain that we will come out of this admittedly complicated phase better than we went into it."[6]

But emotion could not be banished so easily from the public sphere. Growing up, Merkel had been able to draw the line between what she could prove, and therefore knew to be fact, and what she had been taught or told by the Communist state. Now, the power of social media and having an emotion-driven leader in the White House made it more difficult to challenge narratives, stories, and ideas, even if they could not be proven. She had been a target of it herself, with theories about alleged cooperation with the authorities in her youth circulating online and published in books. Yet Merkel knew that she had withstood the pressures of growing up in a dictatorship by knowing which red lines she would never cross. She wouldn't cooperate with the secret police, the Stasi, back in those days. Now, she wouldn't feed the forces at work to undermine the democracy that she had spent half her life dreaming of and the other half working to uphold and improve for the next generation.

In December 2020, even as she gave in to the passion she felt for the situation, pleading with Germans to understand that meeting as a family over the upcoming holidays risked making it the last celebration they would have with elder members, she reminded them that her appeal found its basis in fact:

"The fact that Europe is where it is today is thanks to the Enlightenment and the belief that there are scientific findings that are real and that it is better to stick to them."[7]

Chapter 9

UNFAZED BY BULLIES

When men evolve, it's the natural course of things.
But when a woman asserts herself in politics,
there are murdered men all along her path.

—ANGELA MERKEL

It started the moment she entered politics. Not just the focus on her appearance, but the remarks about how "tough" she could be but at the same time so charming. The shock when she fired a key aide without consulting any of the men around her. Then came the coup, her public calling out of Helmut Kohl, her mentor and political father.

He had plucked her from obscurity and handed her a ministry, granting her legitimacy in a party system buttressed by old boys' networks, that often prized loyalty above competence. Instead of celebrating the competence of a politician with the daring to call things as she saw them and take charge to turn around a negative situation, Merkel became the offender. The German media cast her as a murderess and accused her of patricide or likened her to a hunter.

The German media also likened Merkel's relationship to the men around her to the venomous spider known to eat her partners after mating, the black widow. At a carnival parade in 2018, one of the most popular political floats carried a giant head with Merkel's face attached to eight hairy legs. A trickle of blood oozed from its lips, the figure enthroned over a jumble of bones inscribed with the names of some of her male counterparts. Merkel had no comment. In refusing to discuss her relationship to men, she practiced her own version of Michelle Obama's declaration "When they go low, we go high."

In the early 2000s, Germany still felt to a young American woman like a country stuck in the 1950s. A man who sat in the newsroom right behind me continued to defiantly light up his cigarillos although I had asked him to stop because I was pregnant. I would often find myself the only woman reporter at a news conference, surrounded by dozens of men. Watching a woman rise above what felt like the constant questioning of whether a woman belonged in a powerful place, whether a newsroom, a background briefing, or the highest levels of national politics, felt reaffirming. From her earliest press conferences, Merkel came across as honest and down-to-earth. She answered reporters' questions directly—even if she would insist on the right to alter what she told you. I remember noting her even tone, her dry humor, and her willingness to be very open when she knew she wouldn't be quoted. Unlike previous politicians I covered, Merkel's responses, even if she was dodging a question or repeating one of her well-known phrases instead of giving the detail you sought, were always respectful. She did not treat journalists as if we were the enemy. She treated us with respect.

DON'T FEED THE TROLLS

The backdrop could not have been more beautiful, or more typically German. From the stage at the far end of a cobblestoned market square lined with trim houses painted in pale pink and yellow, the hills of Saxony could be seen rising up in the distance. As Angela Merkel took the stage, an earsplitting noise of air horns and whistles broke the peace, rising above signs held aloft reading MERKEL IS NOT MY CHANCELLOR! and

MERKEL MUST GO! Gripping the microphone, Merkel gazed out over the crowd. But instead of addressing the detractors, she acted as if they were not there. She had decided to hold a rally in the town, deep in the region where the Alternative for Germany party held sway over voters, egging them on against her and her policies. She knew many people opposed her decision to allow hundreds of thousands of migrants into Germany. But she refused to back down from her belief it had been the right move, even if it meant trying to deliver her stump speech over the cacophony of anger and aggression trying to drown her out.

Merkel's party won the election with the highest number of votes, although the Alternative for Germany, or AfD, also entered the German parliament, as the largest party in opposition to the government. That position is crucial in Germany's multiparty system, as its role is seen as keeping the government in check. Instead, the members of the AfD used their platform to continue heckling the chancellor throughout her final four years in office. Merkel's response—though criticized by some as inadequate and fueling the popularity of the nationalist, populist party—was to maintain her cool demeanor and use every opportunity she could to fight their roil of raw emotion with hard, cool facts. After the AfD was accused of accepting illegal donations, its leader used the lectern in parliament to defend herself, veering from the agenda, which called for debating the proposed federal budget. When it came Merkel's turn to speak, she opened by remarking coolly, "The beauty of democratic debates is that everyone talks about what they think is important for the country."[1]

Fighting back against emotion using facts and pointing out the obvious became Merkel's default way of trying to disarm the AfD during her final years in office. At a public event hosted in her home constituency, another member of the party showed up and took a seat in the front row. When it came time to ask the chancellor questions, he opened by giving his opinion that she had with her open-door migration policy turned Germany "into a dictatorship" that was worse than what they had experienced during East German times. Merkel sat calmly and listened to him as he listed his complaints. When he had finished speaking, she picked up her microphone and smiled. "That you are here in the first row and face no danger by asking your question speaks for itself," she replied, over mounting applause from the audience.[2] Merkel's personal motto from her earliest days in politics had been that power is found in the peaceful depths of remaining calm. She not only repeated that idea to anyone who would listen, she lived it.

TURN A THREAT INTO
AN ALLY INTO A FRIEND

When a young senator from Chicago wanted to use the Brandenburg Gate for a foreign policy speech during his 2008 campaign for the presidency, Angela Merkel's position was clear: the right to speak at the monument in central Berlin that symbolized like no other the city's division and reunification had to be earned. Presidents spoke there, not candidates. "No German candidate for high office would think to use the National Mall or Red Square in Moscow for a rally, because it would be seen as inappropriate," the chancellor said through a spokesman. The Gate would have to wait. Instead, Obama was allowed to speak a mile away, beneath the golden Goddess of Victory, who stood atop a column built to celebrate Germany's victories against its neighbors in the nineteenth century. More recently, it had served as the beating heart of reunified Berlin's party scene, from techno raves in the 1990s to the heart of celebrations during the 2006 soccer World Cup.

Obama's speech on a bright, hot July afternoon fit right into that vein, attracting some two hundred thousand people eager to catch a glimpse of the ambitious young senator. Merkel, who had welcomed him to her office for a brief meeting just before the speech, watched it from afar. Obama's speech drew on Berlin's history of overcoming division, Obama speaking in soaring terms of "our destiny" and "improbable hope"—all themes that any German politician would be laughed at for bringing up. Coming from an American, and the first person of color who would be nominated by a major party to run for the highest office in the United States, the speech was lapped up by the crowd. Merkel was jealous that he could speak so eloquently that he was able to attract such a large crowd, a former aide told me. She was impressed, but also annoyed. But once he became president of the United States, she knew there would be no place for such grievances. Still, she went into their first meeting with her guard up.

Obama had chosen Buchenwald, the former concentration camp—not Berlin—for his first visit to Germany as president. His great-uncle had taken part in the liberation of a subcamp of Buchenwald in April 1945. Merkel convinced Obama to also make a stop in the nearby city of Dresden. During a press conference there, I remember the stiffness as they stood side by side, each gripping the edges of their respective lectern. Obama sought to shoot down questions of their strained relations as "wild speculation." Afterward they visited the city's Lutheran cathedral, which had been reduced to rubble by Allied bombers during World War II and rebuilt after reunification, funded in large part by donations from the German diaspora in the United States. There, under the soaring bell-shaped dome, he made his first move, whether intentional or not, to break the ice. He decided to test the acoustics. "He came in here and started singing spirituals," Merkel said. "That was quite fantastic."[3] It was after the Group of 20 meeting in Cannes in 2011, when Obama and Sarkozy pushed Merkel past her limit before pulling back, that their friendship seemed to solidify. Obama eventually took her side in the dispute of that meeting, and the chancellor realized that he was a leader who really listened to her and took in what she was saying. The two also recognized in the other someone who had a similarly dedicated, intellectual, and fact-based approach to their jobs.

"When she would travel to Washington, he would greet her and say, 'I hope you had a good journey,' then they would get right down to business. There was never any small talk or chitchat about what they did on their time off, they would just dive right into it," Klaus Scharioth, who served as the German ambassador in Washington from 2006 to 2011, told me. "That was different than with Bush, when they would talk about all kinds of things before getting to the heart of the matter."[4]

Months before the G20 meeting, Obama had awarded Merkel the Presidential Medal of Freedom, the United States' highest civilian honor and one of the most important to Merkel, among the dozens of recognitions she has received. Obama said the medal was an expression of how much he valued Merkel and her political commitment to freedom and multilateralism. Accepting the award with a toast at a state dinner, held in the Rose Garden of the White House before some two hundred guests, the normally reserved chancellor seemed almost giddy. She returned the favor by allowing him in 2013, as President Obama, to hold a speech in front of the Brandenburg Gate.

From then, their relationship underwent the usual strains of differences over policy and approaches to problem-solving on the global stage. Obama still needed Germany to increase spending on its military and defense, and his administration swiftly joined with Poland, the Baltic states, and others in Europe condemning construction of a second undersea natural gas pipeline linking Russia to Germany, Nord Stream 2. But worst of all, in 2013, the fiercely private Merkel learned that the U.S. National Security Agency had been tapping her private cell phone for years. An outraged German public debated the issue for months. After chiding Washington and expelling the head of the CIA mission in Germany, Merkel instead turned her energies to trying to close what she realized had become a dangerous gap in the differences between the digital abilities of the United States and Europe. Above all, she sought to diffuse the situation by personally refusing to compare the tapping to the threat posed in her past by the all-knowing East German secret police, the Stasi.

In the years that followed, the crises continued to pile up. Russia annexed Crimea, then more than a million migrants entered Europe. In

between, yet another installment of Europe's debt crisis left the two leaders realizing that the importance of the guiding principles they shared
outweighed the differences they encountered. Obama would often defer
to Merkel in dealing with Vladimir Putin, letting her speak to the Russian president about ideas that she and Obama had discussed. He encouraged Merkel to take the lead in negotiations for a cease-fire after
Russian troops marched into Crimea in 2014 and began backing a sepa-
ratist region on the country's eastern border with Russia. The following
year, Obama backed the Paris Agreement, helping Merkel to achieve her
dream of seeing a global agreement to reduce climate-killing gases.

Throughout it all, they kept talking. By the time he left office, Obama
featured at the top of Merkel's list of weekly calls. She spoke to Obama
regularly and he would defer to her on a lot of questions about who
among international players should be included. She turned to him for
support on issues of democracy and help in rallying key players to get
behind policies she needed to push through among other Western leaders. As they worked together, their mutual appreciation grew. Each came
to recognize in the other an intellectual equal, and a fellow outsider who
had broken a mold by being elected to office. They shared a similar,
analytical approach to problems and an unwavering belief that their own
personal success, and that of the two powerful democracies that they led,
depended on a continued respect for the rule of law and fair elections.

By Obama's final years in office, their relationship had deepened beyond that of a typical working partnership. In 2015, a photo of the two of
them during the Group of Seven summit in Bavaria, him sitting relaxed
on a wooden bench overlooking the Alps, she with arms spread out in
an open gesture of explanation, made headlines around the world. They
looked like the old friends that they were, able to exchange ideas with a
level of comfort that had been unthinkable when Obama first came to
office. The following year, the president returned to Germany, this time
to Hanover, to open a trade fair that is the pride of German industry.
While there, knowing that he had a captive German audience, he used

the opportunity to defend his friend and her policies on immigration. "By the way, what's happening with respect to her position on refugees here in Europe—she is on the right side of history on this," Obama told the crowd. "And for her to take on some very tough politics in order to express not just a humanitarian concern but also a practical concern, that in this globalized world, it is very difficult for us to simply build walls, she is giving voice I think to the kinds of principles that bring people together rather than divide them.[5]

That trip was supposed to be Obama's last to Germany. But after Trump's victory at the ballot box, Obama decided to return to Berlin for a farewell tour. One evening Merkel invited the leaders of Britain, France, Italy, and Spain to join them, and another night, at his request, she invited a select group of friends to the chancellery. But the night he arrived, just the two of them met at the Hotel Adlon, two doors down from the U.S. embassy and overlooking the Brandenburg Gate—by now not just a symbol of a reunited Berlin, but the start of their friendship. They talked for three hours. It was during that trip, knowing that President Trump would pursue a profoundly different agenda from that Obama and Merkel had embraced, that Obama urged Merkel to accept the mantle that she had always claimed she did not want, the standard-bearer for the democratic world order. Months earlier, he had told reporters he did not envy Merkel her ability to remain in office as long as voters chose to keep her there. But at the end of his final trip, he had changed his mind. Knowing the respect that her levelheaded, well-informed approach to leadership garnered around the world, he bluntly stated, "If I were here and I were German, and I had a vote, I might support her."[6]

Obama reserved his final call to a foreign leader before leaving the White House for Merkel, thanking her for eight years of friendship and wishing her "the very best going forward."

FIGHT FIRE WITH RESOLVE,
AND FACIAL EXPRESSIONS

Angela Merkel's ability to say what she was thinking without uttering a word was so legendary that the British comedian Tracey Ullman created an entire sketch around the power of the chancellor's eye roll. It shows Merkel, played by Ullman, being flipped off a sofa and onto the floor, while concentrating on not allowing her eyes to roll to the back of her head as President Trump speaks, insisting that Germany owes the USA money. "I kept my eyeline straight, but my powerful eye muscles flipped my entire body instead," the frustrated Merkel declares.[7] Made the year that Trump took office, the parody foreshadowed how the chancellor would manage not to betray her outward composure, while making sure the public knew she had thoughts about the U.S. president. Over the next four years, she let her face do the talking when dealing with Trump. Whether drawing her brows in confusion or befuddlement, or boring through him with her exasperated poker face—she usually tried to keep the eye rolls to a minimum, although she got caught on camera giving one to Putin in 2017—Merkel made sure to use every means she had to relay the danger she believed that Trump posed to the international world order and democracy in his own country.

Trump's victory caught Berlin off guard, leading Merkel's government scrambling to find contacts within the new administration. The day that Trump was elected, Berlin wondered how the chancellor would react. As one world leader after the other published congratulations over social media, she remained silent. Merkel had never been one to race to put out her opinion, but this time the world grew impatient waiting to hear what she would say. Even before taking office, Trump was taking shots at Merkel, belittling her policies and generally demeaning Germany. While many of these shots had been fired over social media, Merkel had never responded to them personally, only occasionally allowing a member of her staff to counter falsehoods with fact. The day after the election was no different. The chancellor, knowing her words would carry weight and set the tone for the four years that lay ahead, chose her words carefully. And when they were ready, she chose to deliver them personally.

When she announced she would make a statement at the chancellery, her staff and aides—normally invisible to the journalists who come to hear her statements—lined the railings of the mezzanines that ran around the atrium that serves as a press auditorium to hear her speak. Everyone knew that Merkel, and her open-door immigration policy, had been a favorite target of Trump's during the campaign. He lashed out at her being named *Time* magazine's 2015 Person of the Year. Celebrated as the "Chancellor of the Free World," Merkel became the first woman to carry *Time*'s honor in nearly two decades, "for asking more of her country than most politicians would dare, for standing firm against tyranny as well as expedience and for providing steadfast moral leadership in a world where it is in short supply," the magazine said.[8] Merkel, who had her hands full trying to convince her country and its European partners that the nearly 1 million people could successfully be integrated into the Western value system and way of life, barely acknowledged the award at the time. But Trump seethed, calling Merkel the "person who is ruining Germany."[9]

But no matter what he threw her way, Merkel had refused to engage. Now she had no choice. Merkel used the opportunity to lay down the ground rules for how she envisioned the German-American relationship going ahead. "Germany and America are bound by common values— democracy, freedom, as well as respect for the rule of law and the dignity of each and every person, regardless of their origin, skin color, creed, gender, sexual orientation, or political views," she said, speaking in the even tones that she chose for occasions when she knew her words would be weighed carefully. "On the basis of these values I offer the future president of the United States, Donald Trump, close cooperation."[10]

Her first phone call with the new president lasted about five minutes, just long enough to leave an impression that maybe the two leaders could find common ground. After all, the closeness that she shared with Obama had only come several years into their relationship, after an awkward and prickly start. She set about trying to understand the man whom neither she nor anyone on her team had ever met, poring over all of the books, interviews, and even TV shows that he had starred in, steeling herself for what she might encounter. An initial meeting, in Washington, was planned for the spring.

She had her staff boil down stacks of files to bullet points, charts, and maps to make them easier for him to understand, knowing he did not like to read. She brought the top bosses of German companies doing business in America along with her, with the aim of impressing on the new president the economic importance of free trade and the two countries' shared ties. None of it worked.

When they appeared alongside each other in the Oval Office, Trump stared straight ahead as the photographers asked for a handshake—the trademark photo of bilateral state visits. Merkel leaned over and quietly asked the president if he wanted to have a handshake. He refused to even look at her, rubbing his hands together before him instead. Merkel leaned back with a cock of her brow, a bemused smile, and a shrug. At the press conference that followed, she kept up a brave face. As he criticized Germany for failing to pull full weight in NATO and taking advantage of the United States in trade deals and took a swipe at her refugee policy, Merkel would not be drawn out. Her pointed response: "It's always much, much better to talk to one another than about one another."[11]

The visit answered any questions Merkel might have had about whether her rocky start with Trump could be turned around, especially after he pulled the United States out of the Paris Agreement—since her days as environmental minister in 1994, Merkel had worked to get the world's leading industrial countries, especially the United States, on board with an international agreement to cut greenhouse gases. From there, the relationship became one of necessity. She would work together with Trump on the most pressing issues while growing into her role as the voice of free trade, multilateral cooperation, and liberal democracy. Trump became the only U.S. president not to make a state visit to Berlin, despite two trips to Germany, once for the Group of 20 summit in Hamburg in 2017 and two years later, on a stopover to greet U.S. troops stationed at Ramstein Air Base. Merkel returned the favor by flying directly in and out of Boston in May 2019, giving the commencement address at Harvard University without visiting Washington.

In that speech, Merkel flashed her ability to speak between the lines, a survival skill that she had learned as a freethinking girl growing up in a dictatorship. She did not mention the U.S. president once by name but urged graduates to "tear down walls of ignorance." To their credit, despite being raised in a democracy the audience recognized what they were hearing was a takedown of Trump's America First brand of politics and a rousing cry for democracy. They responded with a standing ovation.

WHEN ALL ELSE FAILS, KEEP TALKING

Vladimir Putin was president of Russia when Angela Merkel took office, and when she stepped down from power sixteen years later. Of all world leaders she dealt with regularly he remained the most constant, and the most constantly frustrating. The two shared similar backgrounds, both raised in socialist systems, she in the former East Germany and he in the former Soviet Union.

But 1989–90 drove a wedge between them. He believed his nation had lost influence and respect on the world stage. She believed her country had gained freedom, but learned through that event to respect change and, in many cases, avoid provoking it.

Fast-forward to 2014, after half a dozen phone calls to Moscow that saw her position harden from one of warning him to avoid "any step that could contribute to escalation" to bluntly telling him that his plan to hold a referendum in Crimea over whether it should join Russia was "illegal." Realizing that Putin was not backing down and staring at the possibility of the first full-scale military conflict in Europe since the bloody and brutal breakup of the former Yugoslavia, Merkel held fast. She imposed economic sanctions on Russia and supported excluding Putin from the Group of Eight, composed of the world's leading industrial powers, with annual summit meetings, which Russia had been invited to join in the early 1990s, after the collapse of the Soviet Union.

Still, Merkel knew that just because she and Putin had opposing views about many things, from the outcome of the end of the Cold War to the United States' influence over the European Union, which he saw as manipulated by Washington, Russia remained too great a player and a power to simply be ignored. Germany's economic ties with Russia reach back centuries. Gratitude for Moscow's agreement to withdraw troops from the former East German territory and allow for the reunification of the divided nation runs deep in many corners of the country. Given their shared history and geographical proximity, Russia was a partner that she had to deal with. Even if that meant putting up with Putin's power plays and belittling shenanigans. "It was completely clear to me that we were dealing with someone who does not wish us well," she recalled. "But I can't just get rid of him."[12]

In the tense days that followed the annexation of Crimea, when Merkel struggled to rally many member states of the European Union to unite behind economic sanctions against Russia, a fellow European leader recalled marveling at how, despite realizing that Putin had lost all respect for her, she refused to close the door to him. When asked about it, the German chancellor replied that she was willing to be humiliated by Putin if it meant keeping the peace in Europe.

Even after a first attempt at a cease-fire in eastern Ukraine had collapsed and as leaders in Kyiv begged for more weapons to steel themselves against the advance of Russia's powerful military, Merkel sought to avoid an armed conflict. She likened the situation in eastern Ukraine to the construction and subsequent collapse of the Berlin Wall and made clear she was willing to wait the situation out. At the time, most Germans deeply opposed any action that would even appear to involve arming Ukraine. Merkel, raised under the shadow of the threat of war between the United States and the Soviet Union, did not want to be the chancellor who allowed a return to armed conflict in Europe. "I understand that many people are worried about a military confrontation. That is why I have ruled out military intervention from the outset and am working for a diplomatic solution," she said, articulating her response to Moscow's action, which included supporting a raft of sanctions that proved deeply unpopular with many Germans, including in her party and the country's eastern states, as well as its European partners.

"We will have to have staying power. The division of Germany also existed for forty years, was never accepted by the old West German Republic, and was peacefully overcome in the end.[13]

The Germans have a word, *Sitzfleisch*, quite literally "seat meat," but meaning the ability to outlast negotiating partners. Merkel had this quality in spades, not only in her ability to remain at the table until a solution had been found or a conflict resolved, but in her occupancy of the chancellery. By the time she left office at the end of 2021, she had worked with four U.S. and four French presidents, five prime ministers from Britain, and eight from Italy. The only leader who had been in office at the start of her first term and was still there when she left—albeit with a four-year hiatus—was Vladimir Putin. "Merkel had a very realistic view of him," a senior German official who had been involved in supporting German-Russian economic interests told me. "She understood him, and he had tremendous respect for her."

That respect wasn't always obvious. Putin would leave her waiting, often up to an hour. He would lecture her on what was wrong with Germany and launch into grand speeches. Merkel would, at most, roll her eyes. If really angry, she might publicly chide him over his country's lack of civil society during a joint press conference before journalists. But most of the time, she simply accepted his bullying as what it was—the result of the training of an elite officer of the Soviet secret service. Putin had spent several years stationed as a KGB officer in Dresden in East Germany.

After one of her first encounters with Putin, before she had become chancellor, Merkel joked to her aides that she had passed the "KGB test" by holding his gaze steadily without lowering her eyes. Ahead of their first official meeting in the Kremlin, Merkel let her team know that she had a bad history with dogs and did not like being around them. After she arrived, Putin came up and said, "I hear you have a problem with dogs," and handed her a large stuffed dog as a gift.

Two years later, as the two leaders sat before journalists in Putin's residence in Sochi, a door opened, and Koni, the Russian president's big black Lab, wandered into the room and over to Merkel. The chancellor stiffened, her legs tightly crossed, and eyed the Russian president, who sat with his legs splayed widely, seeming to struggle to repress a smile as the dog settled calmly at the chancellor's feet. After the incident, she told reporters, she understood he had to pull such a stunt, "to prove he's a man."[14] She took the tactic in stride. Drawing from every lesson she had learned as a child growing up in a dictatorship, where she had been taught to read and speak between the lines, she knew better than to let him see her sweat. Behind closed doors, to her closest circle, she could complain and let free the frustration and anger that she felt toward the man who seemed intent on humiliating her in public. But she knew that to let him see emotion of any kind would be letting him get the better of her. "A brave chancellor has to cope with a dog," she said. "If such psychological problems mean that you are no longer capable of acting, then something is going wrong."[15] From Putin, she had to cope with more than just the dog. Hackers, assassins, and a steady beat of propaganda accompanied her throughout her final years as chancellor. She made sure that Putin never felt isolated and, at the same time, never got the better of her.

Merkel's ambivalence toward Russia would remain a constant force in her foreign policy and a source of frustration with Washington. Especially her willingness to go ahead with a second undersea pipeline, Nord Stream 2, a year after Russia annexed Ukraine and sent troops into eastern Ukraine. Obama warned that the pipeline could create a dangerous dependence on Russia, and President Trump decried the project, joined by a noisy chorus of Germany's allies in Eastern Europe. Merkel, her government, and Germany's powerful industrial leadership all willfully ignored the naysayers. Not the repeated breaking of a cease-fire agreed to in Ukraine, not a murder committed by a Russian agent less than a mile from the chancellery, not the poisoning of Russian opposition leader Alexei Navalny, whom Merkel had brought to Berlin for treatment, could change the chancellor's mind. She kept talking to Putin, and he kept the gas flowing.

Even her friends view her actions critically. "Angela Merkel could have tried to free the German economy from this dependency since it is the only real leverage that Europe had against Putin," Hillary Clinton said."[16] Instead, Merkel's government allowed the Russians, through local subsidiaries of Russia's state-owned energy giant Gazprom, to buy up miles of Germany's gas pipeline network as well as several of the facilities that are used to store natural gas in the summer for use in the winter.

Merkel has conceded that Europe should have taken the threat posed by Russia more seriously in 2015. But her focus had been on the delicate balancing act of keeping Putin engaged, out of fear that if he was isolated—as happened during the months of the coronavirus pandemic, leading up to his February 2022 full-scale invasion of Ukraine—he would be even more dangerous. By the time that she was concerned about increasing aggression from Moscow, it was too near the end of her term in office. During her final visit to Moscow, she said, it was clear to her that she had broken another barrier in German politics, this time by becoming the country's first lame-duck leader.

"In summer 2021, after President Biden met with Putin, Emmanuel Macron and I had wanted to put together a productive negotiating format in the EU Council," she said. "Some were opposed to the idea, and I no longer had the power to push it through, because everyone knew I'd be gone that autumn."[17]

When she pressed leaders from other European Union countries to take a stand, they demurred, she said, saying that either the problem was too large or the countries they came from too small. Had she been running for reelection, she said that she would have pushed hard, would have followed up. But as the situation stood, everyone knew that her days were numbered and her leverage on the world stage had been spent. The Russian president made sure she realized that he understood her new, weakened position when she traveled to Moscow for her farewell visit. His message, she said, was unmistakable: "The feeling was quite clear: 'You're done with power politics.' For Putin, only power counts."[18]

Before Merkel, no German chancellor had willingly ceded power. They had either lost an election or a vote of confidence on the parliamentary floor. No other chancellor had gone through an extended period—several years in Merkel's case—when it was widely known when the chancellor would leave. Here again, Merkel broke a mold. She demonstrated her belief that the power she held had only been loaned. It was the German people who had returned her to office four times for sixteen years and ultimately held power, not their elected leader. The idea of challenging that would never occur to her. She also believed that a democracy lives from change. Germany, she knew, needed to move on. So did she.

Chapter 10

LEAD WITH STEADFAST COMPASSION

*It goes without saying that we will help
them and take in people who seek refuge here.*

—ANGELA MERKEL, 2015

In the pictures, Angela Merkel is always smiling. Gone is the stern look and the thick lines of her jowls. Her chin is slightly raised, her gaze a soft mix of wistfulness and hope. "Merkel we love you" and "Compassionate mother" read the inscriptions below the portraits, which flooded social media sites in the Arabic-speaking world in 2015. It was the year that would change so much for the German chancellor, the year that she would rewrite the historical image of Germany. A nation still marked with the shame of having driven citizens from its borders in cattle cars would come to be seen as one that welcomed foreigners fleeing war and conflict. Merkel's decision to keep Germany's borders open to the masses, even as Hungary, Denmark, and other countries closed theirs, would earn her criticism at home and abroad. It would stoke the smoldering nationalist sentiment among those Germans who felt their hard-earned fortunes were being sacrificed to provide for the new arrivals. But Merkel's decision, and her subsequent refusal to back down from it, even as Germany fell victim to acts of terror and the backlash grew fiercer, cemented her role as an icon.

Merkel's swift decision to take in and integrate more than a million people who came from an entirely different culture, and most of whom practiced a different religion, earned her accolades from leading universities, including Harvard and Johns Hopkins. Moral leaders, including Pope Francis, praised her "humane and sustainable" version of politics and held her up as a role model.[1] But it was the former prime minister of New Zealand who homed in on how the legacy of Merkel's decision in 2015 spoke volumes about who she was at the core of her being. It singled her out as "a true leader," Jacinda Arden said, "but also just a very good person."[2]

KEEP TRYING, EVEN WHEN IT HURTS

As her motorcade sped from the airport to the center of Athens in the fall of 2012, a mob broke through the cordons of riot police, pelting her black sedan with bottles. Outside the parliament building, she was met by tens of thousands of protesters who had poured into the streets, some brandishing a giant banner reading MERKEL RAUS, German for "Merkel get out." Others waved pictures of her dressed in the drab brown shirts of the Nazi uniform, or with her image doctored to show her hair slicked back and a toothbrush mustache bristling beneath her nose. The message was unmistakable: in the eyes of the Greeks, the demands she had made and continued to make of them were equivalent to the atrocities committed in Greece and across Europe by Adolf Hitler.

If Merkel felt hurt, angry, or insulted, she did not let it show. Her decision to go to Greece had been driven by the idea of showing solidarity with the people there, of acknowledging their hurt and suffering, to keep the European project from falling apart. No one, it seemed at the time, was happy with her effort. Not the Greeks, the Germans, or even many of Germany's partners, who considered Merkel's insistence on austerity too demanding and harsh. But Merkel refused to cede her resolve that the outcome would, over time, be worth the sacrifices made in the moment. "I am aware that the situation is tough," she told the Greek president. "I am here to support Greece."[3]

It would take a long, painful decade of rebuilding and restructuring before the Greek economy would return to stable growth. By the time Merkel left office, no one in Europe questioned the country's viability within the bloc. Many young Greeks who remembered the violent protests against austerity and the impact it had on their families and lives are intent on building a more stable, sustainable future for their country. But they are not the only ones who carry memories of that upheaval. When asked a decade later to look back and assess what had been her most challenging moment throughout her career of crisis management in Europe, Merkel singled out the protests in Greece. Although she had remained stoic at the time, she had not been impervious to the blame that Greeks had pinned on her. She knew that she had been asking a lot of the people of Greece, but she had also asked a lot of other Europeans. She had been intent on finding a solution. That people had interpreted it instead as an insult, blaming her personally for their economic pain and suffering, had stung. "My picture appeared in many facets as the evil woman," she recalled. "That was difficult."[4]

The woman frequently dubbed the Iron Chancellor had a softer core than she allowed most people to see. The longer she stayed in office, the more it became visible.

BE TRUTHFUL TOWARD OTHERS
AND BE HONEST WITH YOURSELF

What began on a Wednesday afternoon in July 2015 was supposed to be a routine town hall exchange with students at a middle school in the northeastern port city of Rostock. It would end in one of the worst public relations disasters of Merkel's terms in office, throwing the fact-based leader from the security of data into the tumultuous world of human emotions that can surge to the surface of teenagers. But the events of that day would also be seen as the spark that informed the defining moment of her terms in office, when she decided several months later to keep the German border open for hundreds of thousands of people escaping war and conflict. It began with a discussion on immigration.

Reem Sahwil, a fourteen-year-old, had come to Germany with her family for medical treatment for physical disabilities that had plagued her since she was born. Once in Germany, her physical health improved. She was able to attend school, got good grades, and was elected the speaker of her class, the same class that was to meet the chancellor. Clutching the microphone that afternoon, she told Merkel that her life's goal and dream was to go on to college in Germany. But her family was not sure if they would be allowed to stay in the country. The limbo left her disheartened, she said. "It's really hard to see how others can just enjoy life and know you can't enjoy it the same way," Reem told the chancellor, whose palms were pressed together tightly between her knees.[5]

Since the start of that year, tens of thousands of people had begun arriving in Germany, most of them fleeing the bloody conflict in Syria. Germans angry that their country was taking in ever more people whom they saw as a threat had been gathering in the streets of Dresden on Monday nights, decrying what they saw as an "Islamization of Europe." But immigration was not the only topic keeping the chancellor awake at night that year. A new Greek government opposed the strict financial conditions agreed to by its predecessors in exchange for more money to service its debts. Now, after the other European countries had decided to keep the Greeks in the common currency, Athens was threatening to pull them out. Merkel's closest advisers estimated that in the spring of 2015 more than 70 percent of her time had been spent trying to save Greece and the euro from the latest threat of collapse.[6]

Only forty-eight hours before she had set off to the school, Merkel had pulled one of the all-night sessions around the negotiating table in

Brussels for which she had by then become known. Well past midnight, when her colleagues would retreat to their office couches to catch a few hours' sleep, leaving an aide at the table in their stead, Merkel would hold on. Draped in a blanket to ward off the chill of the air-conditioned room in the early-morning hours, Merkel would keep pulling leaders aside, sounding them out to find a compromise. A lost night's sleep had left bags under her eyes, but not for a moment did she consider canceling her visit to the school.

When Merkel agreed to attend an event, she showed up. She would carefully weigh the stacks of invitations that landed on her desk to address groups or visit factories or institutions, choosing those she deemed worthy of her time or able to carry her message. She prided herself on keeping her word and maintaining her reputation as reliable. She also knew that a last-minute cancellation might have raised speculation about her health and stamina. After a decade in office—and still undecided whether she intended to seek a fourth term—the last thing she wanted was speculation over whether she was still up to the job. On top of all that, she knew that the students and their teachers had spent weeks preparing for and getting excited about her visit. Tired or not, she did not want to disappoint them.[7]

But whether Merkel had spent an equal amount of time in preparation was another question. Not that she didn't have her facts straight. After Reem had earnestly explained her dream, Merkel quizzed her on where her family had come from and what their legal status was in Germany. Reem explained that they were Palestinians who had been living as refugees in Lebanon before they had been allowed to come to Germany, where they were still waiting for a decision on whether they would be granted permanent asylum and allowed to stay. Merkel listened intently. Then she responded, "I understand that, and yet, politics is sometimes hard."

Then gesturing toward the girl with the long, wavy dark hair pulled back from her face, Merkel smiled softly and held out her hand in a gesture of openness, telling Reem that she came across as extremely nice.

But there were laws that had to be respected and upheld, Merkel said, insisting that Germany couldn't take in all the refugees living in camps from Lebanon to Africa. "We just can't manage that," she told the girl in the same tone that she used when speaking to fellow politicians and policymakers. "There will be some who have to go back."[8]

Looking out at the students, seated in rows of wide benches before her, Merkel continued her explanation as if she were speaking before parliament. Then abruptly, she stopped. Leaning slightly to the right, Merkel's face softened, as if it suddenly hit her that the people before her were young, bursting with dreams that rode on a roller coaster of emotion. As usual, Merkel had pored over the data and prepared her talking points. But she had somehow failed to connect with the emotional impact of the moment, until it was too late. Across from her, the teenager desperate to remain in Germany was struggling to fight back tears. A friend slid closer and protectively pulled Reem, who was now collapsing into full-blown sobs, into a supportive hug.

"Oh, come," Merkel said, smiling sympathetically, as Reem sought to choke back sobs. "You did a great job." The chancellor made her way to the girl and reached out to stroke her hair.

"I don't think it's about doing a great job, Madam Chancellor," the moderator interjected. "It is a very stressful situation."

Turning to him sharply, Merkel snapped. Her mother liked to tell the story about how, as a girl, young Angela had a hard time standing up for herself. She liked to keep the peace. But one day, the boy seated at the desk behind her pushed her too far with his teasing, and she turned abruptly and smacked him good and hard. Looking back on the situation, she recalled the feeling of only having two emotional levels, equanimity or anger, with no steps in between. Those of us who followed her for the press rarely saw her displays of temper, but others who had witnessed it knew it could be fierce.

"I know it is stressful!" Then Merkel leaned back over Reem, her hand on the girl's shoulder, trying to calm her. But the girl continued sobbing as Merkel kept trying to comfort her, saying, "You did a great job explaining for very, very many others what kind of situation you can find yourself in, right?"

It was the first time most people had seen Merkel interacting with a child. Despite being called *Mutti*, she had decided early in her career that she could not balance politics with raising children and remained childless. Her husband had two sons, whom she knew and whose children she would vacation with, but none of those relationships were ever made public. Unlike the practice of U.S. presidential candidates or congressmen and women, who hoist their children into their arms onstage or bring them to witness the signing of key legislation, children are largely absent from German politics. Merkel would speak to school groups, but this was the first time that such a meeting had veered off script, into the realm of emotion. Seeking to regain control of the situation, Merkel returned to the front of the room and shifted back into political mode. It was one of the few times that I can recall seeing her at a loss. She began listing off the decisions her government had taken to address the growing numbers of people who were making their way to Germany. But this time, the facts were not helping.

Within hours, a clip of Merkel leaning over the sobbing girl had whipped around social media. People leaped on the chancellor's behavior as indicative of her coldness, her lack of empathy, and her government's overall inability to respond to a problem that affected the lives of millions of people who did not have the privilege of being born into the affluence of modern Germany. In the feeding frenzy of the criticism that rained down on Merkel in the weeks that followed, the only person who defended her was the girl who had been so upset that day, Reem.

In dozens of interviews with German and international press, she insisted that Merkel had shown interest in her family by asking detailed questions about their situation and legal status in the country. Merkel had also responded truthfully, Reem said. "She was honest, and I find that good," the girl told my *New York Times* colleague, who interviewed her days after the encounter.[9] Merkel later invited Reem to the chancellery for a personal meeting. Merkel refused to say much about their meeting and had instilled in the girl the rule of privacy, so Reem did not say much either. But the girl indicated that it had been a warm second encounter and appreciated Merkel's taking time out of her schedule to sit down with her. Several years later, Reem made headlines again, in 2017, when she was granted asylum and the right to remain indefinitely in Germany.

Merkel did not speak of the encounter again. But several weeks later, when faced with the dreams of many thousands of more people who were turning to her with the same hope as the young teen, the chancellor found a different message. Instead of stressing what Germans could not manage, as she had initially done in speaking with Reem, she chose a different path. Faced with reports of the men, women, and their children who had fled the armed insurgency in Syria that had descended into a bloody civil war, she insisted they be allowed to enter the country. When other leaders in Germany and Europe questioned her decision, she stood firm. Drawing on the lessons of history, she reminded Germans of the difficulties that they had overcome, first after the devastation of World War II, then again when knitting together two formerly opposed countries. The arrival all at once of so many people needing shelter, food, and health care presented a similar challenge, she said, one she was sure that Germany could manage as well as it had managed those in the past. When critics questioned her decision, she stood firm in her belief that the only response could be a humanitarian one.

CHALLENGE YOURSELF, AND OTHERS, AND BE SURPRISED AT WHAT YOU CAN DO

Weeks later, Germany's Federal Office for Migration and Refugees posted a directive on the social media site Twitter. The seventy-seven-character note sounded as dry and bureaucratic as the office that posted it, and for several days not many Germans took note. Even those of us tasked with parsing the flurry of government messages coming our way largely glanced over what sounded like several lines of standard-issue German bureaucratese. But the message would prove to have a butterfly effect that set in motion a course of events that would change the face of Germany and the rest of Europe.

It would also change how the world saw Germany and its leader, Angela Merkel, previously revered for her stoic pragmatism and dedication to upholding the status quo, whatever the cost. Overnight, she had become a model humanitarian, willing to bend the rules that no longer fit the desperation of the moment. A woman who had escaped Syria with her two sisters told me that she felt personally grateful to Merkel for taking the risk to allow them into the country. Walking hundreds of miles to reach Germany, the woman had kept a picture of the chancellor in her pocket, she said, taking it out to kiss it at the start of every day.

"#Dublin proceedings for Syrian nationals are largely de facto not being pursued by us at this time," read the message, posted on August 25.[10] What it meant was that Germany, already overwhelmed by the number of people arriving in the country to claim asylum, would exempt Syrian nationals from the European Union rule requiring migrants to submit their application with the authorities in the country where they first set foot in the bloc. Put more bluntly, Syrians arriving in Germany from Greece, Hungary, Italy, or whichever country was their port of entry would not be turned back. They could stay.

By the time the terse official statement reached the cell phones of people desperate to escape the threat of Islamic extremists or the brutality of Syrian president Bashar al-Assad's police, it had been translated from German into Arabic or English and back again, like a global game of telephone. Many Syrians, desperate to escape the bombing of their homes and threats to their families, read the message as an open invitation. As far as they were concerned, the migration office might as well

have written, "Germany welcomes Syrians." Only the Germans themselves seemed unaware that an invitation had been extended.

By the final week of August, an estimated fifty thousand people had
reached the grand nineteenth-century train station in the heart of Budapest, the Hungarian capital. They had made their way largely on foot
from Greece to Macedonia, then on through Serbia's fields. They slept
huddled together under open skies, relying on handouts from volunteers
for food along the way and chargers to power their cell phones, which
served as maps, compasses, and information boards. At the Hungarian
border, they had risked their lives climbing through the fence reinforced
with razor wire strung up that summer to prevent people from illegally
entering the country. Their plan was to catch trains from Budapest that
would carry them west into Austria, then on to Germany. Chanting
"Germany, Germany" and "Merkel, Merkel," they made it clear where
they wanted to go.

Hungary's prime minister, Viktor Orbán, prevented them from leaving. Trapped in a country where the migrants knew they were not welcome and had no desire to stay, they grew angry, frustrated, and restless.
Footage of the chanting crowds reached Germany. So, too, did images
of exhausted mothers clutching their sleeping children and fathers hov-
ering over dozens of family members crammed together in unsanitary
conditions. To many, the sight seemed hauntingly familiar. In the plight
of the Syrians, Germans saw the crimes of their grandparents, mirrored
back at them in a modern sheen. The desperation etched on the faces of
the migrants recalled how the Nazis had rounded up Europe's Jews and
left them suffering in train stations, before loading them onto cattle cars
bound for extermination camps.

When she took her seat in the press auditorium of the chancellery
behind the long bench where the guests sat before a bright sky-blue wall,
Merkel remarked that it was the final day of summer in the meteorologi-
cal calendar, August 31. Her hot-pink blazer with a subtle silver necklace
transmitted a message of cheerful confidence, even as behind the scenes

the pressure was mounting for her to intervene to diffuse the mounting tensions at the train station. Merkel did not wait for the journalists' questions. She had come armed with a plan and quickly laid out how her government would provide for and integrate these people who were intent on making Germany the center of a new life.

Merkel had spent years thinking about and finding hope in the German constitution, or Basic Law, with its core values of the protection of human dignity and human rights. For the first thirty-five years of her life, those guarantees had provided her comfort, knowing that if the pressure of life in a dictatorship ever became unbearable, she could cross into West Germany, where their protection would be extended to her. The people now trying to reach Germany held the same hope and longing for safety. To deny them these rights would be a betrayal of that document she held in such high regard. Merkel also knew that basic human rights, including the right to asylum, are enshrined in the European Union's Charter of Fundamental Rights. In the early years of her chancellorship, she had negotiated for the charter to come into force. And she knew that Germany, perhaps more than any other in Europe, had a moral obligation to uphold respect for human dignity.

After laying out the facts and acknowledging the challenge that would come with accommodating so many people, Merkel summed up the situation with a message of confident encouragement: "The motto with which we approach this must be, we have achieved so many things, we can do this [*wir schaffen das*]."[11]

The impact of the three German words flew past many of us crammed elbow to elbow in the seats of the auditorium that Monday afternoon. Only a few of the leading German newspapers or broadcast channels mentioned it the next day in their reports of the chancellor's press conference. But as the summer turned to fall, with thousands crossing into Germany each day, the phrase would come to be seen as the overarching definition of Merkel's leadership during that time, both from those who supported and those who opposed her policies.

Days after expressing her confidence that Germany could handle the challenge posed by the migrants, the Hungarian prime minister decided that if the people wanted to march to Germany, he would not stop them. Hundreds of people set off on foot toward the Austrian border. Their final destination was Germany. When Merkel got the call that the march was underway, she had only hours to decide how to respond. The Austrian chancellor had let her know that people were on the move. He feared that the only way they could be stopped was by force.

The last time she had been confronted with such a situation, Merkel had been on the other side. On the night of November 9, 1989, determined East Germans had begun their march to West Berlin. The border guards had been trained to shoot anyone seeking to cross without a visa. Had any one of them opened fire that night, the peaceful revolution that led to German reunification and Merkel's own personal freedom and rise to power might never have happened. A quarter century later, Merkel found herself in the same position the East German authorities had been in that night. Trying to close the German border would mean violence. Tear gas would be turned on innocent civilians, parents carrying their children among them. Images of Hungarian police beating back people at their border had caused outrage across the globe. Merkel understood the power of pictures. She knew the devastating impact that images of German police attacking refugees would have.

For a leader known for deliberating and turning over every option before making up her mind, the situation could not have been worse. It was a Friday evening. Tens of thousands of people had already left Hungary, making their way toward the southern German border. "The refugees were on European ground and were standing in front of our doors. And to say, 'Look, go back over the Mediterranean,' was not an option," she later recalled.[12]

Even if she had already decided to allow the refugees to cross the border, she still had to consult with her ministers. They had all scattered for the weekend, and her interior minister, responsible for the country's security, was in bed sick. Her vice-chancellor and the minister for the economy, Sigmar Gabriel, was sitting at home with his family when Merkel called. She told him that she wanted to allow fifteen thousand people from the train station in Hungary to enter Germany, despite their having no visas and, in many cases, not even passports. He agreed immediately, but warned that the move should be an exception. Hours later, crowds of cheering Germans flooded the Munich train station to greet the exhausted migrants who had boarded trains in Vienna. Waving flags and hand-drawn signs welcoming people in slogans in Arabic, English, and German, they chanted, "Say it loud, say it clear, refugees are welcome here!," and sang songs. Bewildered but relieved to have reached Germany, the weary travelers accepted the food, teddy bears, and bottles of water handed to them as they made their way to the reception centers where they would be registered and given a bed and a medical checkup.

Those images of a joyful welcome went around the world. Merkel's grand gesture, echoed in the smaller gestures of individual Germans, sent a message that the chancellor was willing to risk her political capital in the name of standing behind her beliefs.

When she met that night with key members of her governing coalition, her interior minister was still angry. More than ten thousand people were arriving in Munich daily. The discussions about how to handle the arrivals wore on well past midnight. When they finally broke, around three or four o'clock in the morning, Merkel spoke to her vice-chancellor to make her conviction perfectly clear. "We went out and Angela Merkel pulled me aside and said, 'Promise me one thing, Mr. Gabriel,'" he recalled the chancellor telling him. "'We won't build any fences here in Germany.'"[13]

Merkel had made up her mind how the country she was leading should respond to the unprecedented situation. Mindful of German history and with the same deep conviction that had allowed her to climb the ranks of the powerful West German conservative party to become the first woman, the first former East German, and the first trained scientist to lead first the Christian Democratic Union and then the government, Merkel doubled down on her position that Germany, and Germans, were capable of receiving and integrating the hundreds of thousands of people still making their way to the country. As the numbers of new arrivals grew, so did the critics. Integrating so many people at once strained communities and even the most dedicated volunteers. Some Germans resisted the new arrivals with violence, setting fire to shelters prepared to house them and attacking buses carrying them into their communities.

Merkel remained firm in her conviction that Germany could manage the challenge. She visited shelters and posed for selfies with—mostly male—arrivals, who beamed with pride that their journey had not only brought them to the safety of Europe's economic powerhouse but afforded them a chance to stand beside the woman they credited with making their arrival possible. Merkel's critics swiftly and loudly decried her outreach efforts as painting a disingenuous picture that would only encourage ever more people to come to Germany, already straining to accommodate hundreds of thousands. As the pressure mounted, she remained firm in her conviction. She pointed to the many thousands of Germans who had turned out to assist, in ways large and small. They had set up beds, doled out food, and donated clothing and supplies. In doing so, they changed the way the world saw their country. "I have to say quite honestly, if we now have to start apologizing for showing a friendly face in emergency situations, then this is not my country," Merkel insisted.[14]

But that friendly face came at a price. The following year began with sexual assaults by migrant men against hundreds of German women in Cologne. Months later, a young Afghan severely injured several passengers with an axe in a train, and within days another newly arrived young man attempted to blow up a quiet Bavarian town square. The brutal year of 2016 culminated in a Tunisian man's seizing a truck and deliberately driving it into a Berlin Christmas market, killing twelve and injuring more than fifty others. When Merkel succeeded in her attempts to bring her European partners around to accepting more refugees, she agreed to a deal under which the European Union paid Turkey billions of euros to close off its borders, preventing more people from heading north. Critics charged that Europe was leaning on Turkey to do its dirty work, but Merkel understood that she had asked as much as she could of Germans. The country's capacity had been exhausted.

A LIVING LEGACY OF COMPASSION

Before leaving office, Merkel never liked to talk about her legacy. While still chancellor, she insisted that every day in office demanded her full attention. She would contemplate what came next after she had left. Germany's former chancellors don't build libraries or set up foundations, as U.S. presidents do. Their paths once leaving office have been varied: one became copublisher of a leading weekly newspaper, another set up a consulting firm, and still another has become a member of the boards of leading Russian energy companies.

After leaving office, Merkel first took time off to contemplate what she wanted to do with the next chapter of her life. She has refused, despite pressure from at home and abroad, to get involved over the war in Ukraine, insisting that her time in office is done. She has stood by her decisions as having been made with the best intentions and information that she had at the time. She is writing her political memoirs to explain her positions. Above all, she is exploring what life outside politics could look like for her, someone who has done nothing but politics since 1989. "I never had the opportunity to ask myself what would be the most interesting other than politics," she said. "At sixty-seven, I don't have an endless amount of time. So I would like in this next phase of life to consider very carefully what do I want to do."[15]

After writing her political memoirs, what Merkel will do remains unclear. But her legacy has already begun to emerge.

By the time she stepped down in late 2021, more than two-thirds of the "new residents" that she had welcomed into the country were working full-time, paying taxes, and contributing to German society.[16] Many were becoming eligible for citizenship, changing the face of their new-found country's future. That same year, among the thousands of children who started first grade in schools across Germany were hundreds of children born to Afghans, Iraqis, Nigerians, and Syrians whose parents had arrived in Germany between 2015 and 2016. Among them were dozens of little girls named Angela and a few boys called Merkel and even the odd Angela Merkel. They will carry her name into the future, serving as a living legacy.

ACKNOWLEDGMENTS

This book would not have been possible without the support of many kind and generous people who believed in the project and my ability to see it through to the end.

Special thanks to Julia Cheiffetz for deciding this book needed to be written and agreeing that giving it up when the war broke out would be letting the men win. Thanks to the team at One Signal and Simon & Schuster, including Abby Mohr and Kathleen Rizzo, and to Sean deLone for his enthusiasm, humor, and patience in editing. Thank you to Susan Canavan, my agent, for finding me and sticking with me from the lockdown days through the outbreak of full-scale war in Ukraine.

Among the friends who never wavered in their support for me, I thank Marla Luther for her political insight, essential points on style, and critical levity at times of crisis; Kirsten Grieshaber and Ze'ev Avrahami for believing in this book from before it was born; and John Goetz for convincing me to keep going when I was ready to give up. Thank you to Jennifer Flock for providing me with a lifesaving writer's retreat and to Clarissa Jacobson for her endless enthusiasm and reminding me to always dream big. *Danke* to Michael Fischer for the notes, details, and willingness to keep talking Merkel long after she had left the front page.

I thank Amy Anderson-Habig for her careful readership, Tara Eddy for being my cheerleader, and Katja Schulze-Brüggemaann, Alison Smale, Amanda Bower, Joshua Hammer, Sudha David Wilp, Hannah Cleaver, Jill Mazullo, Lucian Kim, Alan Chin, Derek Scally, and Shane MacMillian for sharing their thoughts over dinners and discussions along the way.

Thanks to my colleagues, especially Jack Ewing, Nicholas Kulish, Guy Chazan, Matt Anderson, Katrin Bennhold, and Christopher Schuetze, along with all my editors at the *New York Times* for their advice and patience with me during this project. My gratitude to all of my German colleagues, whose writings and work helped make my own research much easier.

To Paul LaFarge, who advised me that it is only worth writing a book about Merkel if it is a good one; I miss you and I hope that I have succeeded.

I am grateful to my dad, Donald Eddy, and my siblings, Amy, Jennifer, and Steve, for making me who I am today. Mom would be proud of us all. To Jacob and H.J., thank you for putting up with my absences, making your own dinners so I could write, and answering my messages with Merkel stickers.

NOTES

INTRODUCTION

1. Christine Lagarde, "Laudatory Speech by Christine Lagarde, President of the ECB, for Angela Merkel at the Award Ceremony for the North Rhine–Westphalia State Prize," May 16, 2023, https://ecb.europa.eu/press/key/date/2023/html/ecb.sp230516-f6f9794177.en.html.
2. Angela Merkel, "Speech by Dr. Angela Merkel, Chancellor of the Federal Republic of Germany, on the Occasion of the 368th Harvard University Commencement on May 30, 2019, in Cambridge, MA," Harvard University, May 30, 2019, https://www.bundesregierung.de/breg-en/service/archive/speech-by-dr-angela-merkel-chancellor-of-the-federal-republic-of-germany-on-the-occasion-of-the-368th-harvard-university-commencement-on-may-30-2019-in-cambridge-ma-1634366.
3. Annette Schavan, *Die hohe Kunst der Politik* (Freiburg im Breisgau, Germany: Verlag Herder, 2021), 13.

CHAPTER 1:
EVERYTHING I DO, I DO AS A WOMAN

1. Angela Merkel, "Inspiring Women: Scaling Up Women's Entrepreneurship," W20 Germany Summit, April 25, 2017, https://video.bundesregierung.de//bpa/2017_g20/2017-04-25-streaming-merkel-w20-dialogforum-OT_HQ.mp4.
2. Angela Merkel, "Angela Merkel & Chimamanda Ngozi Adichie in Conversa-

tion with Miriam Meckel & Léa Steinacker," Düsseldorfer Schauspielhaus, September 13, 2021, https://www.youtube.com/watch?v=A035X2LKAnM.

3. http://www.frauenhintermerkel.de/.

4. "Historical Data for the Percentage of Women," IPU Parline, Global Data on National Parliaments, Germany, Bundestag, https://data.ipu.org/node/65/data-on-women?chamber_id=13316.

5. "Monthly Ranking of Women in National Parliaments," IPU Parline, Global Data on National Parliaments, https://data.ipu.org/women-ranking?month=11&year=2021.

6. "Gender Equality Index, 2021," European Institute for Gender Equality, https://eige.europa.eu/gender-equality-index/2021/country/DE.

7. Norbert Lammert, "Plenarsitzung im Deutschen Bundestag AM 11/22/2005," Open Discourse, https://opendiscourse.de/plenarsitzungen/16-3.

8. Angela Merkel, "Rede von Bundeskanzlerin Merkel bei der Festveranstaltung '100 Jahre Frauenwahlrecht,'" November 12, 2018, https://www.bundeskanzler.de/bk-de/aktuelles/rede-von-bundeskanzlerin-merkel-bei-der-festveranstaltung-100-jahre-frauenwahlrecht-am-12-november-2018-1548938.

9. Angela Merkel, "Gender Parity in All Areas Just Seems Logical," interview with Jana Hensel, *Die Zeit*, January 28, 2019, https://www.zeit.de/politik/deutschland/2019-01/angela-merkel-chancellor-cdu-feminism-interview.

10. Alexandra Föderl-Schmid, "Merkel unter Männern," *Süddeutsche Zeitung*, October 8, 2018, https://www.sueddeutsche.de/politik/besuch-in-israel-merkel-unter-maennern-1.4161183.

11. Angela Merkel, "Global Solutions 2018—Q&A with German Chancellor Angela Merkel," May 29, 2018, https://www.youtube.com/watch?v=9YFV1QjC4FA.

12. Angela Merkel, "Diskussion bei 'JugendPolitikTagen': Bedürfnisse von jungen Leuten bleiben im Mittelpunkt," *Die Bundesregierung*, May 7, 2021, https://www.bundesregierung.de/breg-de/suche/jugendpolitiktage-2021-1912090.

13. "Mädel, küß mich: Frauenministerin Merkel will mit einem Gesetz gegen Busengrabscher vorgehen," *Der Spiegel*, 45/1991, November 3, 1991, https://www.spiegel.de/panorama/maedel-kuess-mich-a-ab198d1d-0002-0001-0000-000013490848.

14. Angela Merkel, "Als sie noch von der Macht träumte," *Emma*, May 1, 1993, https://www.emma.de/artikel/angela-merkel-die-toechter-schlagen-zurueck-317079.

15. Melissa Eddy, "Angela Merkel 'Feels Solidarity' for Congresswomen Targeted by Trump," *New York Times*, July 19, 2019, https://www.nytimes.com/2019/07/19/world/europe/angela-merkel-trump-squad.html.

16. Merkel, "Gender Parity in All Areas."

17. Anna Kaminsky, "(Verordnete) Emanzipation?—Frauen im geteilten Deutschland," Bildungszentrale für politische Bildung, March 5, 2019,

https://www.bpb.de/geschichte/zeitgeschichte/deutschlandarchiv/286988/
verordnete-emanzipation-frauen-im-geteilten-deutschland.

18. Ibid.
19. Angela Merkel and Hugo Müller-Vogg, *Mein Weg* (Hamburg, Germany: Hoffmann und Campe, 2004), 112.
20. Franziska Reich, "Wer leiten will muss schön sein," *Stern*, June 18, 2005, https://www.stern.de/politik/deutschland/angela-merkel-wer-leiten-will--muss-schoen-sein-3291166.html.
21. Evelyn Roll, *Die Kanzlerin: Angela Merkels Weg zur Macht* (Berlin: Ullstein Buchverlag, 2009), 172.
22. "Sixt und seine umstrittenen Werbeplakate," *Die Welt*, https://www.welt.de/wirtschaft/gallery119348548/Sixt-und-seine-umstrittenen-Werbeplakate.html.
23. Roll, *Die Kanzlerin*, 177–78.
24. "Panorama: Angela Merkel: Cabrio-Fahrt als Entschädigung," *Der Tagesspiegel*, May 8, 2001.
25. Andreas Maciejewski, "Promifrisör Udo Walz: Angela Merkels Haarschnitt kostet 65 Euro," WEB.DE, November 20, 2015, https://web.de/magazine/unterhaltung/stars/promifrisoer-udo-walz-angela-merkels-haarschnitt-kostet-65-euro-31149736.
26. Matthias Kamann, "Die Bundeskanzlerin ist ein bisschen erstaunt gewesen," *Die Welt*, April 15, 2008, https://www.welt.de/welt_print/article1902405/Die-Bundeskanzlerin-ist-ein-bisschen-erstaunt-gewesen.html.
27. Erik Kirschbaum, "Merkel Tries to Downplay Fuss over Opera Gown," Reuters, April 18, 2008, https://www.reuters.com/article/idINIndia-33113020080418.
28. Rebecca Schuman, "Angela Merkel's Been Wearing the Same Amazing Tunic for 18 Years," *Slate*, August 6, 2014, https://slate.com/culture/2014/08/angela-merkel-has-been-wearing-the-same-tunic-for-18-years-photo.html.
29. Angela Merkel, "Angela Merkel & Chimamanda Ngozi Adichie in Conversation with Miriam Meckel & Léa Steinacker," Düsseldorfer Schauspielhaus, September 13, 2021, https://www.youtube.com/watch?v=A035X2LKAnM.
30. *Süddeutsche Zeitung*, December 2, 2021, https://www.sueddeutsche.de/panorama/angela-merkel-britney-spears-promis-promi-news-1.5478632.
31. Cerstin Gammelin, Nico Fried, and Wolfgang Krach, "Ich weiss was wir geschafft haben," *Süddeutsche Zeitung*, October 22, 2021, https://www.sueddeutsche.de/projekte/artikel/politik/das-grosse-abschiedsinterview-mit-angela-merkel-e623201/.
32. Julian Robinson, "Angela's Walking Wardrobe," *Daily Mail*, August 2, 2017, https://www.dailymail.co.uk/news/article-4752546/Merkel-wears-holiday-outfit-FIFTH-year-running.html.
33. Khuê Pham and Elisabeth von Thurn und Taxis, "Anna Wintour," *Zeit Magazin*, March 20, 2019.

34. Angela Merkel, "Bericht der Vorsitzenden der CDU Deutschlands," Proto-
    koll 22: Parteitag Stuttgart, Konrad Adenauer Stiftung, December 1–2, 2008,
    https://www.kas.de/c/document_library/get_file?uuid=9819cd3e-b9d5-
    75b6-9b82-44cb8b656a80&groupId=252038.

35. "Mutter Angela," *Der Spiegel* 39 (September 19, 2015), https://www.spie
    gel.de/international/germany/refugee-policy-of-chancellor-merkel-divides
    -europe-a-1053603.html#bild-c6806667-0001-0004-0000-000000898422.

CHAPTER 2:
THE ART OF WAITING

1. Gerhard Schröder, *Elefantenrunde 2005*, ZDF, September 18, 2005, https://
   www.zdf.de/politik/unsere-merkel-jahre/berliner-runde-2005-100.html.

2. Herlinde Koelbl, *Spuren der Macht* (Munich: Knesebeck Verlag, Sonderausgabe, 2010), 61.

3. Angela Merkel, "CDU Pressekonferenz," Phoenix, November 20, 2016,
   https://www.youtube.com/watch?v=yX0osniWglA.

4. Judy Dempsey, *Das Phänomen Merkel* (Hamburg, Germany: Edition Körber-
   Stiftung, 2013), 9.

5. Peter Dausend, "Moment des Glücks," *Die Welt*, December 27, 2005,
   https://www.welt.de/print-welt/article186710/Moment-des-Gluecks.html.

6. Koelbl, *Spuren der Macht*, 61.

7. Angela Merkel, "Rede von Bundeskanzlerin Dr. Angela Merkel beim Festakt
   zum Tag der Deutschen Einheit in Kiel," *Die Bundesregierung*, October 3,
   2006, https://www.bundesregierung.de/breg-de/service/bulletin/rede-von
   -bundeskanzlerin-dr-angela-merkel-797168.

8. Angela Merkel and Hugo Müller-Vogg, *Mein Weg* (Hamburg, Germany:
   Hoffmann und Campe, 2004), 82.

9. Angela Merkel, "Die von Helmut Kohl eingeräumten Vorgänge haben der Par-
   tei Schaden zugefügt," *Frankfurter Allgemeine Zeitung*, December 22. 1999.

10. Evelyn Roll, *Die Kanzlerin: Angela Merkels Weg zur Macht* (Berlin: Ullstein
    Buchverlag, 2009), 107.

11. Angela Merkel, "Was also ist mein Land?," Modiertes Gespräch mit Alexander
    Osang," June 7, 2022, https://www.buero-bundeskanzlerin-ad.de/termine
    /und-quot-was-also-ist-mein-land-und-quot/.

CHAPTER 3:
KNOW WHERE YOU COME FROM

1. Angela Merkel and Hugo Müller-Vogg, *Mein Weg* (Hamburg, Germany:
   Hoffmann und Campe, 2004), 43.

2. "1954 werden Tausande Menschen," Jugendopposition in der DDR, January
   1, 1954, https://www.jugendopposition.de/chronik/?_y=1954.

3. Evelyn Roll, *Die Kanzlerin: Angela Merkels Weg zur Macht* (Berlin: Ullstein Buchverlag, 2009), 15.

4. "Angela Merkel in Oberlinhaus 2017," Oberlinhaus, November 13, 2017, https://www.youtube.com/watch?v=eEQZD9TgnuA.

5. Merkel and Müller-Vogg, *Mein Weg*, 38.

6. Angela Merkel, "Flüchtlingsheim Heidenau: Besuch von Angela Merkel am 26.08.2015," Phoenix, August 8, 2015, https://www.youtube.com/watch?v=H3CWeqLkgb8.

7. "Angela Merkel in Oberlinhaus 2017."

8. https://www.bundeskanzlerin.de/bkin-de/aktuelles/rede-bundeskanzlerin-merkel-vor-dem-kongress-der-vereinigten-staaten-von-amerika-319718.

9. Herlinde Koelbl, *Spuren der Macht* (Munich: Knesebeck Verlag, Sonderausgabe, 2010), 49.

10. Gerd Langguth, *Angela Merkel* (Munich: Deutsche Taschenverlag, 2005), 49.

11. Merkel and Müller-Vogg, *Mein Weg*, 68.

12. Angela Merkel, "Abschied von einem Freund der Deutschen," December 5, 2018, https://www.bundesregierung.de/breg-de/suche/abschied-von-einem-freund-der-deutschen-1556370.

13. MAZ/dpa, "Angela Merkel in ihrer Heimat Templin," *Märkische Allgemeine*, September 10, 2021, https://www.maz-online.de/brandenburg/angela-merkel-in-ihrer-heimat-templin-hier-komme-ich-her-hier-sind-meine-wurzeln-PESNVQT67W2WH57EWG5VSXAXK4.html.

CHAPTER 4:
DON'T LET LIMITATIONS STOP YOU FROM LIVING

1. Katja Gloger, *Putins Welt* (Munich: Piper Verlag, 2017), https://specials.dekoder.org/merkel-russland-putin.

2. Angela Merkel, "Die Queen bei der Kanzlerin, " *Der Spiegel*, June 24, 2015, https://www.spiegel.de/video/queen-in-berlin-merkel-fuehrt-elizabeth-ii-durch-kanzleramt-video-1587762.html.

3. Angela Merkel, "Speech by Dr. Angela Merkel, Chancellor of the Federal Republic of Germany, on the Occasion of the 368th Harvard University Commencement on May 30, 2019, in Cambridge, MA," Harvard University, May 30, 2019, https://www.bundesregierung.de/breg-en/service/archive/speech-by-dr-angela-merkel-chancellor-of-the-federal-republic-ofgemany-on-the-occasion-of-the-368th-harvard-university-commencementon-may-30-2019-in-cambridge-ma-1634366.

4. Angela Mekel, "Günter Gaus in Gespräch mit Angela Merkel," *Zur Person*, October 28, 1991, https://www.youtube.com/watch?v=EEY15eXSWgc.

5. Herlinde Koelbl, *Spuren der Macht* (Munich: Knesebeck Verlag, Sonderausgabe 2010), 50.

6. Annette Schavan, interview with author, December 6, 2021.

7. Donald Trump, Twitter, June 18, 2018, https://twitter.com/real DonaldTrump/status/1008696508697513985.
8. Megan Garber, "How 'Badass' Became a Feminist Word," *Atlantic*, November 22, 2015, https://www.theatlantic.com/entertainment/archive/2015/11/how-badass-became-feminist/417096/.
9. Susanne Beyer, "Foto mit Signalwirkung," *Spiegel Biografie* 1/2021, August 9, 2021, https://www.spiegel.de/politik/deutschland/angela-merkel-ein-ur laubsfoto-und-seine-deutung-a-207e1af6-0002-0001-0000-000178572553.
10. Evelyn Roll, *Die Kanzlerin: Angela Merkels Weg zur Macht* (Berlin: Ullstein Buchverlag, 2009), 28.
11. Hubertus Knabe, "IM-Erika: Was ist dran an die Stasi-Gerüchten um Angela Merkel," *Frankfurter Allgemeine Zeitung*, November 6, 2019.
12. Dpa, "Merkel zu DDR-Vergangenheit: Nie irgentwas verheimlicht," *Die Zeit*, May 13, 2013, https://www.zeit.de/news/2013-05/13/film-merkel -zu-ddr-vergangenheit-nie-irgendetwas-verheimlicht-13080605.
13. Angela Merkel, *Was also ist mein Land?* (Berlin: Aufbau Verlag, 2021), 16.
14. Anne Applebaum, "Angela Merkel, the Empress of Europe," *Washington Post*, September 23, 2013, https://www.washingtonpost.com/opinions/anne -applebaum-angela-merkel-the-empress-of-europe/2013/09/23/bb07c81e -247a-11e3-b75d-5b7f66349852_story.html.
15. Barack Obama, "Barack Obama im RTL Interview," *RTL*, November 18, 2020, https://www.rtl.de/cms/barack-obama-im-rtl-interview-ich-sehne -mich-tatsaechlich-immer-noch-nach-change-4652187.html.
16. Merkel, *Was also ist mein Land?*, 17.

CHAPTER 5:
EMBRACE THE POWER OF CHANGE

1. Angela Merkel, "Podiumsdiskussion mit Bundeskanzlerin Merkel an der Prälat-Diehl-Schule in Groß-Gerau," September 30, 2014, https://www .bundesregierung.de/breg-de/aktuelles/podiumsdiskussion-mit-bundeskan zlerin-merkel-an-der-praelat-diehl-schule-845834.
2. Hans-Hermann Hertle, *Chronik des Mauerfalls. Die dramatischen Ereignisse um den 9. November 1989* (Berlin: Ch. Links Verlag, 1999), https://www .chronik-der-mauer.de/material/180368/hans-hermann-hertle-9-november -1989-18-00-uhr-schabowskis-auftritt.
3. Andreas Rinke, *Das Merkel Lexikon: Die Kanzlerin von A–Z* (Springe, Germany: zu Klampen Verlag, 2016), 227.
4. Gerd Langguth, *Angela Merkel* (Munich: Deutsche Taschenverlag, 2005), 61.
5. Ursula Weidenfeld and Katja Weber, "Krisenkanzlerin: Angela Merkel— Zögern, Zaudern und dann springen," *Hörsaal*, Deutschlandfunk Nova, September 12, 2021, https://www.deutschlandfunknova.de/beitrag/angela -merkel-zoegern-zaudern-und-dann-springen.

6. Merkel, "Podiumsdiskussion mit Bundeskanzlerin."
7. Angela Merkel and Hugo Müller-Vogg, *Mein Weg* (Hamburg, Germany: Hoffmann und Campe, 2004), 73.
8. Merkel, "Podiumsdiskussion mit Bundeskanzlerin."
9. Nina Hasse, "How Value Driven Is Angela Merkel? E04. Merkel's Last Dance," Deutsche Welle, January 6, 2021, https://www.dw.com/en/how -value-driven-is-angela-merkel-e04/av-56019712.
10. Dimitri Medvedev, "Speech of President of Russian Federation D. Medvedev at Celebrations Marking the 20th Anniversary of the Berlin Wall's Fall," November 9, 2009, https://russische-botschaft.ru/de/2009/11/11/speech -of-president-of-russian-federation-d-medvedev-at-celebrations-marking- the-20th-anniversary-of-the-berlin-walls-fall/.
11. Alison Smale and Andrew Higgins, "Putin and Merkel: A Rivalry of History, Distrust and Power," *New York Times*, March 12, 2017, sec. A, p. 1, https://www.nytimes.com/2017/03/12/world/europe/vladimir-putin-angela -merkel-russia-germany.html.
12. Vladimir Putin, "Putin to Address Nation: Excerpts," BBC, April 25, 2005, http://news.bbc.co.uk/2/hi/europe/4481455.stm.

CHAPTER 6:
PRACTICE RESOLUTE PRAGMATISM

1. Lara Waas and Berthold Rittberger, "The Berlin Puzzle: Why European Solidarity Prevailed in the Adoption of the Corona Recovery Fund," *European Journal of Political Research*, July 18, 2023, 14, https://ejpr.onlinelibrary .wiley.com/doi/pdf/10.1111/1475-6765.12614.
2. George Calhoun, "Europe's Hamiltonian Moment, What Is It Really," *Forbes*, May 26, 2020, https://www.forbes.com/sites/georgecalhoun/2020/05/26/ europes-hamiltonian-moment--what-is-it-really/?sh=743efa9a1e1a.
3. Dalia Grybauskaitė, interview with author, December 7, 2021.
4. Stefanie Bolzen, "Tony Blair: 'Angela Merkel war richtig für Deutschland,'" *Die Welt*, September 22, 2021, https://www.welt.de/politik/ausland/plus233926158/ Tony-Blair-Angela-Merkel-war-richtig-fuer-Deutschland.html.
5. Ines Pohl, "Bush: Angela Merkel 'Is Not Afraid to Lead,'" *Deutsche Welle*, July 14, 2021, https://www.dw.com/en/george-w-bush-on-angela-merkel-a -woman-who-is-not-afraid-to-lead/a-58249493.
6. "Merkel und Steinbrück in Wortlaut: Die Spareinlagen sind sicher," *Der Spiegel*, October 5, 2008, https://www.spiegel.de/wirtschaft/merkel-und -steinbrueck-im-wortlaut-die-spareinlagen-sind-sicher-a-582305.html.
7. Rainald Becker and Thomas Schneider, directors, *Merkel-Jahre: Am Ende einer Ära, Folge 2*, SWR, October 29, 2021.
8. Angela Merkel, "Regierungserklärung von Bundeskanzlerin Dr. Angela Merkel zu den Maßnahmen zur Stabilisierung des Euro vor dem Deutschen

Bundestag," May 19, 2010, https://www.bundesregierung.de/breg-de/
service/bulletin/regierungserklaerung-von-bundeskanzlerin-dr-angela
-merkel-795942.
9. Peter Speigel, "How the Euro Was Saved," *Financial Times*, May 11, 2014,
https://www.ft.com/content/f6f4d6b4-ca2e-11e3-ac05-00144feabdc0.
10. Spyros Gkelis, Twitter, October 9, 2012, https://twitter.com/northaura/
status/255660515286736896.

CHAPTER 7:
PROTECT YOUR PRIVATE LIFE

1. Angela Merkel, "Angela Merkel und Chimamanda Ngozi Adichie," Düsseldorfer Schauspielhaus, September 13, 2021, https://www.youtube.com/
watch?v=WUVxYtzGGtg.
2. Angela Merkel, "Angela Merkel im Oberlinhaus 2017," November 13, 2017,
https://www.youtube.com/watch?v=eEQZD9TgnuA.
3. George Streiter, "Regierungs Pressekonferenz," April 3, 2013, https://
cvd.bundesregierung.de/cvd-de/pressekonferenzen-briefings/regierungs
pressekonferenz-vom-3-april-846064.
4. *Bild*, August 7, 2014, https://www.bild.de/politik/inland/angela-merkel/
muss-das-wirklich-sein-times-zeigt-kanzlerin-im-badeanzug-37149714.bild
.html.
5. Tracey Ullman, interview with the author, October 14, 2021.
6. Anglela Merkel and Hugo Müller-Vogg, *Mein Weg* (Hamburg, Germany:
Hoffmann und Campe, 2004), 35.
7. Ibid., 115.
8. "Da stimmt die Chemie," *Cicero*, https://www.cicero.de/innenpolitik/da
-stimmt-die-chemie/37140.
9. Herlinde Koelbl, *Spuren der Macht* (Munich: Knesebeck Verlag, Sonderausgabe, 2010), 50.
10. Ibid.
11. Freya Klier, "'Ich will Deutschland dienen.' Bewunderung für eine Regier-
ungschefin," in *Die hohe Kunst der Politik*, ed. Annette Schavan (Freiburg im
Breisgau, Germany: Verlag Herder, 2021), 264.
12. Angela Merkel, "Der Digital-Gipfel 2020: Gespräch der Bundeskanzlerin
mit Miriam Meckel und Achim Berg," January 12, 2020, https://www.bmwi.
de/Redaktion/DE/Videos/2020/Digital-Gipfel/20201201-digital-gipfel
-forum-a-tag2-1325-merkel-interview.html.
13. Koelbl, *Spuren der Macht*, 50.
14. *Bunte*, August 2017, https://www.bunte.de/panorama/politik/angela
-merkel-mein-mann-unterstuetzt-mich-immer-zum-beispiel-indem-er-oft
-fuer-uns-einkauft.html.
15. Anna V. Bayern, Stefan Hauck, and Martin S. Lambeck, "Reise nach An-

geland," *Bild am Sonntag*, September 4, 2009, https://www.bild.de/poli
tik/2009/mit-der-kanzlerin-in-die-uckermark-9413702.bild.html.

16. Gregor Mayntz, "Wo Merkel Kraft schöpft," *Rheinische Post*, July 13, 2014,
https://rp-online.de/politik/deutschland/hohenwalde-wo-angela-merkel
-kraft-schoepft_aid-20308019.

CHAPTER 8:
LEADING AS A SCIENTIST

1. Angela Merkel and Hugo Müller-Vogg, *Mein Weg* (Hamburg, Germany:
Hoffmann und Campe, 2004), 50.
2. Angela Merkel, "Bundeskanzlerin Merkel sieht Licht am Ende des Tunnels,"
December 9, 2020, https://www.bundestag.de/dokumente/textarchiv/2020/
kw50-de-generalaussprache-810038.
3. Bernd Settnik, "Prager Professor erinnert sich: Angela Merkel war stets ruhig
und arbeitswillig," August 25, 2016, https://deutsch.radio.cz/prager-professor
-erinnert-sich-angela-war-stets-ruhig-und-arbeitswillig-8216172.
4. Gerd Langguth, *Angela Merkel* (Munich: Deutsche Taschenverlag, 2005),
181.
5. Greta Thunberg, "Greta Thunberg—wie schaffen wir die Klimarevolution,"
1.5 Grad—der Klima-Podcast mit Luisa Neubauer, Staffel 2, November 2021,
https://open.spotify.com/episode/4hOrkGiMX87T2PWQ82KyTz.
6. "Angela Merkel im Wortlaut: 'Wenn wir nicht gerade aus Stein sind,'" *Der
Tagesspiegel*, September 21, 2016, https://www.tagesspiegel.de/politik/an
gela-merkel-im-wortlaut-wenn-wir-nicht-gerade-aus-stein-sind/14576252
.html.
7. Address to parliament, December 9, 2020, https://www.bundesregier
ung.de/breg-de/service/bulletin/rede-von-bundeskanzlerin-dr-angela-merkel
-1826624.

CHAPTER 9:
UNFAZED BY BULLIES

1. Editorial staff, "So witzig reagiert Angela Merkel auf die Wutrede von Alice
Weidel," *Die Zeit*, November 21, 2018, https://www.zeit.de/zett/politik
/2018-11/so-witzig-reagiert-angela-merkel-auf-die-wutrede-von-alice
-weidel.
2. Angela Merkel, "Merkel erklärt AfD-Politiker was Democratie bedeutet,"
FAZ, August 14, 2019, https://www.youtube.com/watch?v=-zqA2OwhRI8.
3. Andreas Rinke, "Das Merkel-Lexikon: Von Obama über Ost-deutsch und
Privatsphäre bis Queen," RiffReporter: Das Merkel-Lexicon, April 28,
2019, https://www.riffreporter.de/de/gesellschaft/buchstaben-o-p-q-obama
-privatsphaere-queen.

4. Klaus Scharioth, interview with author, July 12, 2021.

5. Barack Obama, "Remarks by President Obama and Chancellor Merkel in Joint Press Conference," White House, Office of the Press Secretary, April 24, 2016, https://obamawhitehouse.archives.gov/the-press-of fice/2016/04/24/remarks-president-obama-and-chancellor-merkel-joint -press-conference.

6. Barack Obama, "Remarks by President Obama and Chancellor Merkel of Germany in a Joint Press Conference," White House, Office of the Press Secretary, November 17, 2016, https://obamawhitehouse.archives.gov/the -press-office/2016/11/17/remarks-president-obama-and-chancellor-merkel -germany-joint-press.

7. Tracey Ullman, "Angela Merkel's Poker-Face Problem," *Tracey Breaks the News*, series 1, episode 1, BBC One, October 27, 2017, https://www.you tube.com/watch?v=p5WPVLljm1A.

8. "Person of the Year: Angela Merkel," *Time*, December 21, 2015, https:// time.com/time-person-of-the-year-2015-angela-merkel-choice/.

9. Donald J. Trump (@realDonalTrump), Twitter, December 9, 2015, https:// twitter.com/realdonaldtrump/status/674587800835092480?lang=en.

10. Angela Merkel, "Pressestatement von Bundeskanzlerin Merkel zum Ausgang der US-Präsidentschaftswahl am 9 November 2016," *Die Bundesregierung*, November 9, 2016, https://www.bundesregierung.de/breg-de/aktuelles/ pressekonferenzen/pressestatement-von-bundeskanzlerin-merkel-zum-au sgang-der-us-praesidentschaftswahl-am-9-november-2016-844040.

11. Angela Merkel, "Joint Press Conference with President Trump and German Chancellor Merkel," Trump White House Archive, March 17, 2017, https:// trumpwhitehouse.archives.gov/briefings-statements/joint-press-conference -president-trump-german-chancellor-merkel/.

12. Angela Merkel, "'Was also ist mein Land?': Altkanzlerin Merkel im Live-Gespräch mit Schriftsteller Alexander Osang," Phoenix, June 7, 2022. https://www.youtube.com/watch?v=hiwnD00kV0w.

13. Angela Merkel, "Podiumsdiskussion mit Bundeskanzlerin Merkel an der Prälat-Diehl-Schule in Groß-Gerau," September 30, 2014, https://www .bundesregierung.de/breg-de/aktuelles/podiumsdiskussion-mit-bundeskan zlerin-merkel-an-der-praelat-diehl-schule-845834.

14. George Packer, "The Quiet German," December 1, 2014, *New Yorker*, https://www.newyorker.com/magazine/2014/12/01/quiet-german.

15. Merkel, "'Was also ist mein Land?'"

16. Diana Zinkler, "Merkel: 'Ich hatte nicht mehr die Kraft, mich durchzuset-zen,'" *Berliner Morgenpost*, November 24, 2022, https://www.morgenpost .de/politik/article236994513/angela-merkel-interview-putin-ukraine-russ land-politik.html.

17. Alexander Osang, "A Year with Ex-Chancellor Angela Merkel: You're Done with Power Politics," *Der Spiegel*, December 1, 2022, https://www.spiegel.de/

international/germany/a-year-with-ex-chancellor-merkel-you-re-done-with
-power-politics-a-f46149cb-6deb-45a8-887c-8aa37cc9b3c3.

18. Ibid.

CHAPTER 10:
LEAD WITH STEADFAST COMPASSION

1. Annette Schavan, *Die hohe Kunst der Politik* (Freiburg im Breisgau, Germany: Verlag Herder, 2021), 13.

2. Shashwat Awasthi, "New Zealand PM Ardern Hails Merkel as 'True Leader,' 'Very Good Person,'" Reuters, November 12, 2021, https://www.reuters .com/world/new-zealand-pm-ardern-hails-merkel-true-leader-very-good-per son-2021-11-12/.

3. Graeme Wearden, "Merkel Visits Greece as 50,000 People Protest—as It Happened," *Guardian,* October 9, 2012, https://www.theguardian.com/ business/2012/oct/09/eurozone-crisis-angela-merkel-visits-greece.

4. Angela Merkel, "Angela Merkel & Chimamanda Ngozi Adichie in Conversation with Miriam Meckel & Léa Steinacker," September 13, 2021, https:// www.youtube.com/watch?v=A035X2LKAnM.

5. Reem Sahwil and Angela Merkel, "Im Dialog mit der Kanzlerin," Gut Leben in Deutschland, July 16, 2015, https://buergerdialog.gut-leben-in-deutsch land.de/SharedDocs/Videos/DE/07-Juli/2015-07-16-dialog-kanzlerin-auss chnitt.html.

6. Andreas Rinke, *Das Merkel Lexikon: Die Kanzlerin von A–Z* (Springe, Germany: zu Klampen Verlag, 2016), 385.

7. Ralph Bollmann, *Angela Merkel: Die Kanzlerin und ihre Zeit* (Munich: C. H. Beck, 2021), 501.

8. Sahwil and Merkel, "Im Dialog mit der Kanzlerin."

9. Jesse Coburn, "Tearful Moment with Merkel Turns Migrant Gril into a Potent Symbol," *New York Times*, July 20, 2015, https://www.nytimes .com/2015/07/21/world/europe/legislation-gives-hope-to-girl-who-shared -plight-with-merkel.html.

10. Bundesamts für Migration und Flüchtlinge, @BAMF_Dialogue, August 25, 2015, https://twitter.com/bamf_dialog/status/636138495468285952?lang =en.

11. Angela Merkel, "Sommerpressekonferenz von Bundeskanzlerin Merkel," August 31, 2015, https://www.youtube.com/watch?v=5eXc5Sc_rnY.

12. Merkel, "Angela Merkel & Chimamanda Ngozi Adichie."

13. Rainald Becker and Thomas Schneider, directors, *Merkel-Jahre: Am Ende einer Ära, Folge 2,* SWR, October 29, 2021, 9:16.

14. Angela Merkel, "Pressekonferenz von Bundeskanzlerin Merkel und dem österreichischen Bundeskanzler Faymann," September 15, 2015, https://www .bundesregierung.de/breg-de/aktuelles/pressekonferenzen/pressekonferenz

-von-bundeskanzlerin-merkel-und-dem-oesterreichischen-bundeskanzler
-faymann-844442.

15. Merkel, "Angela Merkel & Chimamanda Ngozi Adichie."

16. Wido Geis-Thöne, *Eine Bestandsaufnahme fünf Jahre nach dem starken Zuzug*, IW-Report 42/2020 (Cologne: Institut der deutschen Wirtschaft, September 1, 2020), 18.

INDEX

siblings of, 61
silence/guardedness of, 5, 27, 89
sixtieth birthday party of, 78
as a soccer fan, 11
and social media, 80–82
solidarity with women, 27–28
Soviet Union travels of, 70
and the Stasi, 83–86
swimming anecdote told by, 43–44,
 92
vs. Thatcher, 6–7, 104
as *Time*'s Person of the Year, 4–5, 85,
 145
toughness of, 136
on trust, 109
Uckermark country home of, 61–62,
 70, 126–27
United States, fascination with,
 69–70
in *Vogue*, 31
at Waldhof, 60–63, 67, 70, 74
Western ideals of, 66
West German TV watched by,
 66
White House visited by, 58, 69, 124,
 141
on women's rights, 28
as World's Most Powerful
 Woman, 2
Merkel, Angela, as chancellor
 badass status of, 81–82
 on the Berlin Wall's fall, 98, 100
 on the Brandenburg Gate's use,
  139
 Brussels visits, 105
 campaign and election, first, 94,
  97
 campaigns and elections, 6–9,
  18–19, 21–22, 31, 39, 41–42,
  44–45
 at the chancellery, 72
 climate policies of, 131–33, 142
 in coalition negotiations, 45–46,
  74, 79
 conspiracy theories about,
  84–86

coronavirus pandemic, handling of,
 129–30, 133–35
as the Crisis Chancellor, 103–4
decision not to run, 52–53
deliberation and reflection by,
 43–45
democracy promoted by, 1, 58, 90,
 98–99, 142, 147
European debt crisis, handling of,
 110–15
at European Union budget summit,
 105–8
European Union supported by,
 103–5, 112
fact-based approach of, 129–30, 140,
 155–56, 159
female power redefined by, 40
final speech as, 86–89
as first chancellor born after World
 War II, 10, 45
as first chancellor from East
 Germany, 10, 45
as first woman chancellor, 6,
 45–46
on gay marriage, 11, 95–96
Greece visit, 154–55
on the Greek debt crisis, 7, 10, 16,
 103, 111–12 (*see also under*
 Greece)
as a humanitarian, 12, 62, 143,
 160–61
"If the euro fails, then Europe
 fails" mantra of, 112–13
"I. M. Erika" myth about,
 84–85
immigration policy of
 (*see* immigrants to Germany)
"in der Ruhe liegt die Kraft" maxim
 of, 56
as a lame duck, 151–52
legacy of, 167–68
media coverage of, 45–46
on natural gas, 131–32, 141, 151
negotiating skills of, 149
nuclear-power policy of, 94–95,
 102, 131

ABOUT THE AUTHOR

Melissa Eddy is a journalist based in Berlin who covers German business, economics, and politics for the *New York Times*. She covered Chancellor Angela Merkel from the start of her time in office in 2005. A Minnesota native fluent in German and French, she went to Germany as a Fulbright scholar in 1996. Before joining the *International Herald*, in 2012, she was a correspondent for the Associated Press in Frankfurt, Vienna, and the Balkans. *Merkel's Law* is her first book.